Practical
Woodshop Projects

24 NO-NONSENSE PROJECTS TO IMPROVE YOUR SHOP

DANNY PROULX

POPULAR WOODWORKING BOOKS
CINCINNATI, OHIO
www.popularwoodworking.com

Table of Contents

Toolboxes

Workbenches & More

Tool Storage

Machinery Stations

Some Clever Jigs

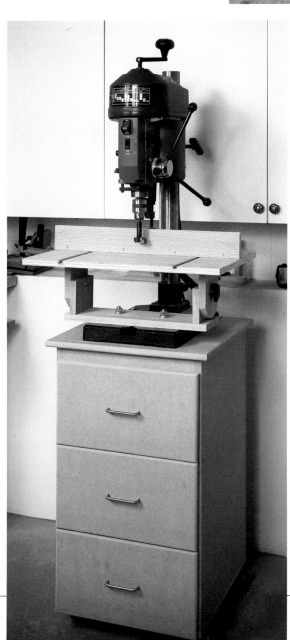

Toolbox Tote

This easy-to-build toolbox tote is a must-have for any wood-worker. It makes all those necessary home repairs a lot simpler because all your tools are close at hand. When friends or family call for help, all you have to do is load up the tote and you're on your way — no running back and forth for another handful of tools.

However, like my friend and editor Jim Stack of Popular Woodworking Books noted in his book *Building the Perfect Tool Chest*, small hand tools usually end up at the bottom of a tote box, making them hard to reach. Jim designed a unique holding system for screwdrivers along the box edges, so I wanted to see if I could also design a possible solution to the problem.

The bottom-mount tray feature is my answer to a small tool storage area that's easy to reach. Simply unlatch the draw catches, and the hand tool tray is released from the main box. All the small tools are clearly visible and easy to reach. The top section of the tote box can be used for levels and carpenter and combination squares, as well as a few small power tools.

This toolbox tote has everything within easy reach, so you don't need to fumble through a pile of tools to get a couple of screwdrivers hidden on the bottom of the box. As we all know, when tools are organized and easy to reach, the project always seems a lot easier. I think you'll find this tote design handy and also a pleasure to use.

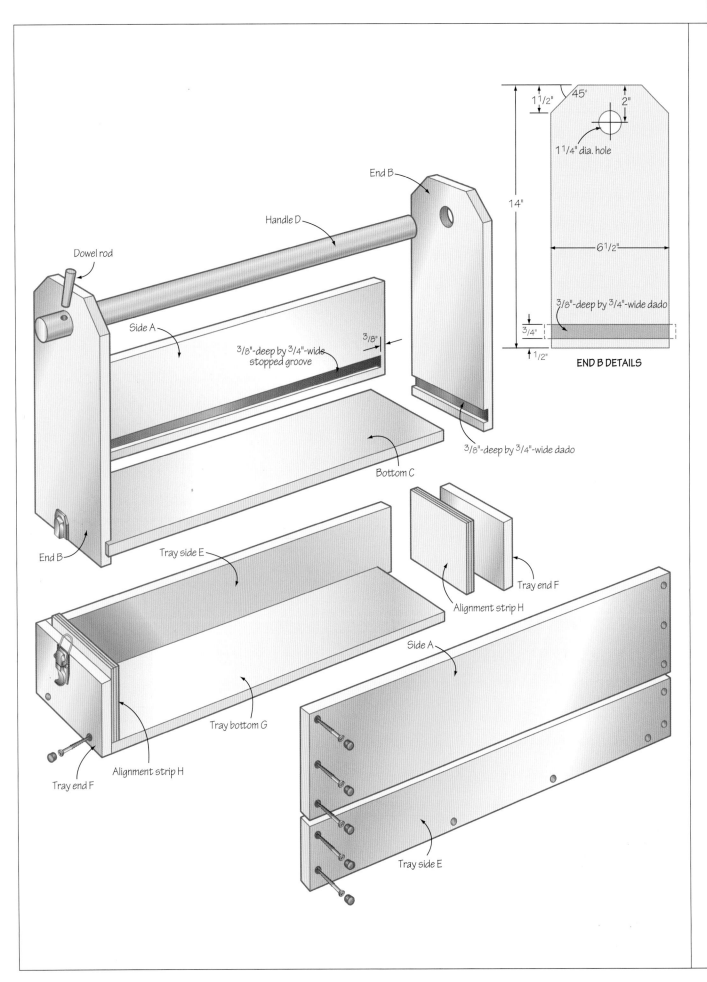

End B

Handle D

Dowel rod

Side A

3/8"-deep by 3/4"-wide
stopped groove

3/8"

Bottom C

3/8"-deep by 3/4"-wide dado

End B

Tray side E

Alignment strip H

Tray end F

Side A

Tray bottom G

Alignment strip H

Tray end F

Tray side E

1 1/2"

45°

2"

1 1/4" dia. hole

14"

6 1/2"

3/8"-deep by 3/4"-wide dado

3/4"

1/2"

END B DETAILS

Schedule of Materials: Toolbox Tote

LTR.	NO.	ITEM	STOCK	INCHES T	(MM) T	INCHES W	(MM) W	INCHES L	(MM) L
A	2	sides	pine	¾	(19)	7¼	(184)	28	(711)
B	2	ends	pine	¾	(19)	6½	(165)	14	(356)
C	1	bottom	pine	¾	(19)	7¼	(184)	27¼	(692)
D	1	handle	hardwood	1¼ dia.	(32)			30	(762)
E	2	tray sides	pine	¾	(19)	3½	(89)	28	(711)
F	2	tray ends	pine	¾	(19)	3½	(89)	6½	(165)
G	1	tray bottom	pine	¾	(19)	6½	(165)	26½	(673)
H	2	alignment strips	plywood	½	(13)	4	(102)	6½	(165)

Supplies

2" (51mm) screws

Nails

Glue

5/16" (8mm) Dowel pins

Mahogany wood plugs

2 Draw catches

STEP 1 Cut the two sides A and two ends B to the sizes indicated in the materials list. The tops of both end panels B are mitered at 45°, 1½" in from each side edge. Clamp the end panels together and ease the sharp corners with a sander. Since the ends are clamped, both will be formed equally and will be identical.

STEP 2 On the inside face of each end panel form a dado that's ¾" wide and ½" above the bottom edge. Each side panel requires a ¾"- wide groove, ½" above the bottom edge. All dadoes and grooves are ⅜" deep. The grooves on the side boards should stop ⅜" short of both ends. This technique is called a blind or stopped groove. The grooves and dadoes can be formed with a router mounted in a table or on a table saw using a dado blade. There are a number of cutting options, but be sure to square the ends of all the cuts to properly fit the bottom board.

SHOP tip

If you can't fully hide a joint, celebrate it, as one longtime cabinet-maker said. To do this I'm using dark mahogany plugs, which are a nice contrast to the light pine boards.

STEP 3 I am using a 1¼"-diameter hardwood dowel rod for my tote box handle D. The dowel will pass through drilled holes near the top edge of each end B. Drill the 1¼"-diameter holes centered on each end panel and located 2" on center below the top edge. Clamp both panels together and drill the holes. Use a piece of scrap lumber under the boards to prevent wood tear-out.

STEP 4 The bottom C is installed in the grooves and dadoes. To allow the wood to expand and contract, don't use glue to secure the bottom. Assemble the tote box and clamp tightly when all the parts are aligned.

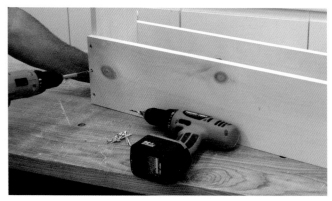

STEP 5 Use three 2"-long screws to secure each corner joint. Counterbore the screw holes, using a ⅜"-diameter counterbore drill bit.

STEP 6 Cut a 1¼"-diameter dowel rod 30" long to create handle D. Drill two ⁵⁄₁₆"-diameter holes through the rod, ¾" on center from each end. Thread the dowel rod through the previously drilled holes in the end boards and drive 2"-long, ⁵⁄₁₆"-diameter dowel pins into the holes on the handle. Use a little glue on each dowel pin, being careful not to glue the dowel rod to the end boards. The tote box will be much easier to lift and carry if the handle rotates freely.

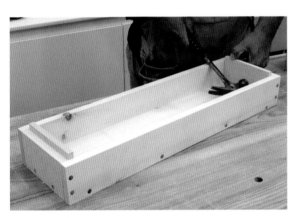

STEP 7 The tool tray is built with the two tray sides E, two tray ends F and the tray bottom board G. Secure the sides and end boards to the bottom board. Use a little glue and 2" screws in counterbored holes. Fill the holes with mahogany wood plugs. The tray should have the same outside dimensions as the tote box section.

STEP 8 Use two ½"-thick by 4"-high pieces of plywood to form the alignment strips H. The strips are glued and nailed in place on each end board. These strips will align the main box to the tray.

STEP 9 Install two draw catches, one on each end of the box, to secure the tray to the main box. Note that the tongue on the top section of each catch should be aligned with the bottom edge of the tote box. If the tongues were below the bottom of the end panel, they might scratch the floor when the tray is removed.

CONSTRUCTION
notes

Apply a finish to the box to complete the project. I used three coats of polyurethane to protect the wood.

This project was built using pine, but just about any solid wood or sheet material will work as well. A solid hardwood box will be more resistant to bumps and dents than this pine box, so if you want that type of durability, use hardwood. Sheet materials, such as ¾"-thick plywood, would also be very strong. Multicore materials such as plywood do not expand and contract as much as solid wood, so all the joints can be glued to strengthen the tote.

You may have specific tool carrying needs, so change the sizes to suit your requirements. If you carry a lot of hand tools, the upper section can be downsized and the tray built deeper. Wood pegs could be added to one side of the box to wrap extension cords that are often needed on the job, or divider slots can be installed in the upper section to keep your tools separated. The options are endless with this great little carrying box.

Carpenter's Toolbox

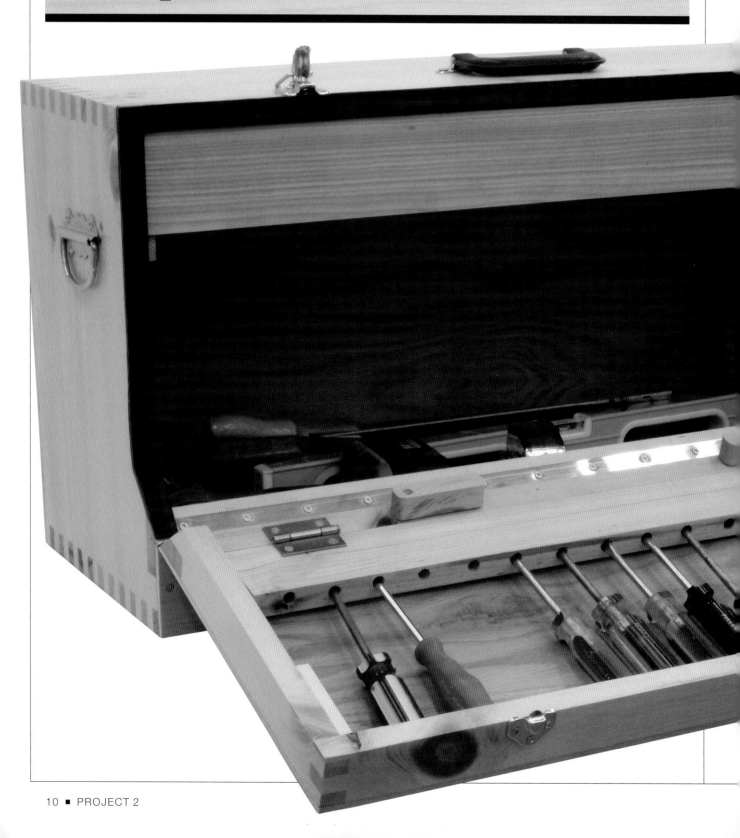

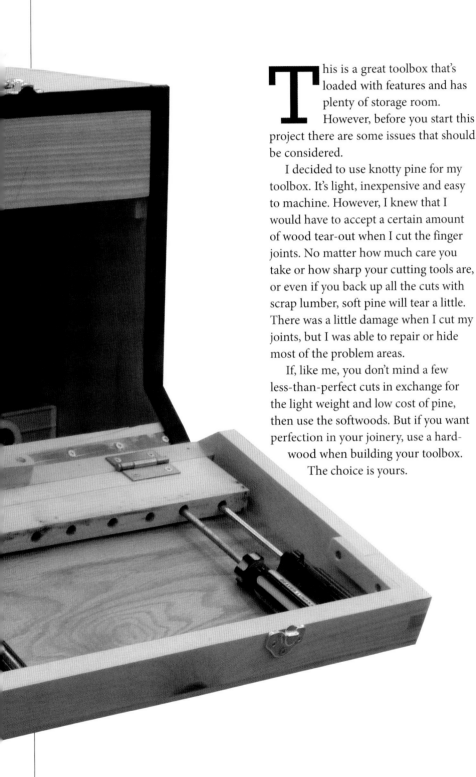

This is a great toolbox that's loaded with features and has plenty of storage room. However, before you start this project there are some issues that should be considered.

I decided to use knotty pine for my toolbox. It's light, inexpensive and easy to machine. However, I knew that I would have to accept a certain amount of wood tear-out when I cut the finger joints. No matter how much care you take or how sharp your cutting tools are, or even if you back up all the cuts with scrap lumber, soft pine will tear a little. There was a little damage when I cut my joints, but I was able to repair or hide most of the problem areas.

If, like me, you don't mind a few less-than-perfect cuts in exchange for the light weight and low cost of pine, then use the softwoods. But if you want perfection in your joinery, use a hardwood when building your toolbox. The choice is yours.

This project is all about box-building using glued-up solid wood and box joints, or as they are often called, finger joints. The sidebar at the end of the chapter details a simple jig you can make for your saw. As I mentioned in an earlier chapter, you should invest in a good carbide-tipped stacked dado blade for your table saw because this is another of its many uses. Give me a table saw with a dado blade and I can build anything.

A carpenter's toolbox can be used to carry hand tools and small electric tools to a work site. The box can be configured in many ways, so think about the tools you travel with most often and customize the interior space to suit your requirements. The large compartment can be used for cordless drills and sanders; the drawer will store chisels and hardware; and the door rack will organize all the screwdrivers you'll ever need on any job site.

Finally, don't be intimidated by the solid-wood glue-up procedures or box joinery. Both are basic woodworking techniques that are not difficult to master. The box joint is used in hundreds of applications and will open the door to many interesting projects. It's sometimes called a poor man's dovetail, but it's a strong, good-looking joint that's used every day in woodshops.

You don't need an expensive jointer or planer to edge-dress solid wood for panels. Acceptable low-cost alternatives are available and I'll detail the options in this project. If you don't need a carpenter's toolbox, there's sure to be a woodworker in your family who would really appreciate this project as a gift.

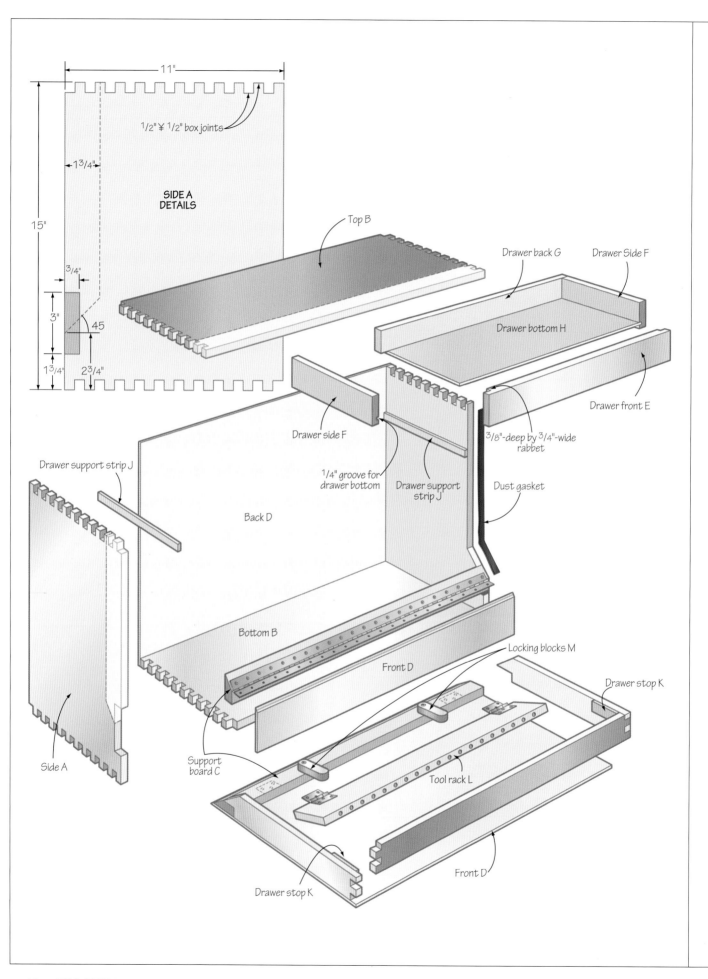

11"

SIDE A
DETAILS

1³/4"

15"

3/4"

3"

45

1³/4"

2³/4"

¹/2" ¥ ¹/2" box joints

Top B

Drawer back G

Drawer Side F

Drawer bottom H

Drawer front E

Drawer side F

1/4" groove for
drawer bottom

Drawer support
strip J

³/8"-deep by ³/4"-wide
rabbet

Dust gasket

Drawer support strip J

Back D

Bottom B

Locking blocks M

Front D

Drawer stop K

Support
board C

Tool rack L

Side A

Drawer stop K

Front D

Schedule of Materials: Carpenter's Toolbox

LTR.	NO.	ITEM	STOCK	INCHES T	(MM) T	INCHES W	(MM) W	INCHES L	(MM) L
A	2	sides	solid wood	¾	(19)	11	(279)	15	(381)
B	2	top and bottom	solid wood	¾	(19)	11	(279)	30	(762)
C	1	support board	solid wood	¾	(19)	3	(76)	30	(762)
D	2	front and back	veneer ply	¼	(6)	15	(381)	30	(762)
E	1	drawer front	solid wood	¾	(19)	3	(76)	28½	(724)
F	2	drawer sides	solid wood	¾	(19)	3	(76)	7⅞	(200)
G	1	drawer back	solid wood	¾	(19)	2½	(64)	28½	(724)
H	1	drawer bottom	veneer ply	¼	(6)	8⅝	(219)	27¾	(705)
J	2	drawer support strips	solid wood	⅜	(10)	¾	(19)	9	(229)
K	2	drawer stops	solid wood	⅜	(10)	¾	(19)	3	(76)
L	1	tool rack	solid wood	¾	(19)	2½	(64)	28	(711)
M	2	locking blocks	solid wood	¾	(19)	¾	(19)	3	(76)

Supplies

Glue

½" (13mm) Screws

¾" (19mm) Brass screws

1" (25mm) Brass screws

1¼" (32mm) Screws

1½" (38mm) Screws

Brad nails

2   3" (76mm) Brass butt hinges

4   Rubber feet

30" (762mm) Piano hinge

2   Chest handles

1   Luggage handle

4   ¼" (6mm) Machine bolts, nuts and washers

2   Draw catches

4' (1219mm) ³⁄₁₆"-thick x ¾"-wide (5mm x 19mm) Weather stripping

STEP 1 The first step is to edge-join enough solid wood to yield the side, top and bottom panels A and B. The edges of each board must be straight to achieve maximum contact when the boards are held together. They can be joined with glue or with glue and biscuits, as I'm doing. Either method is fine. If you don't have a jointer, you can have the lumberyard prepare the boards. However, a well-tuned table saw, with a sharp blade, will cut edges that are acceptable for this type of joinery. Be sure your saw fence is parallel to the saw blade and the blade is sharp. Cut one edge of the board, then flip it over so the cut edge is against the fence and cut the opposite side. Try to maintain an even steady speed when feeding the boards through the saw blade, removing small amounts on each pass. You may have to repeat this step one or two times, but you will get edges that can be joined. Now, edge-join the boards using biscuits and glue or glue only. Clamp the panels together until the glue sets.

STEP 2 Cut the sides A, top and bottom B, and support board C to the sizes listed in the materials list. Arrange the panels so they form the box shape and mark the front face of each board. Use matching numbers on each adjoining face to permit easy assembly once the fingers have been cut.

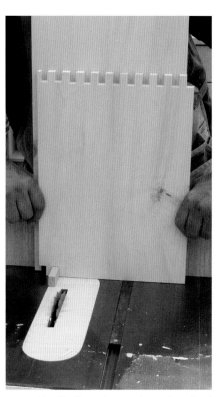

STEP 3 Use the jig and procedures described in the construction notes sidebar at the end of this project to cut the panels. Place the panel faces toward each other when cutting to reduce wood tear-out. I'm using a ½"-wide dado blade setting, which will cut ½"-wide notches and fingers.

STEP 4 Dry fit the box joints and mark the front edges. Take the joints apart and cut a notch on the front edges of the sides A for support board C. This support spans the two sides and will provide a backing for the front plywood panel after the door opening has been cut. The notch is ¾" deep, begins 1¾" from the bottom edge of each side panel, and is 3" wide.

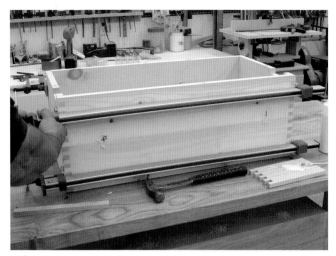

STEP 5 Coat the fingers and slots with glue, then assemble the box. Clamp the joints, making sure the corners are 90° by checking them with a square and moving them into alignment if necessary. Leave the clamps in place until the adhesive cures.

STEP 6 Apply glue to both side board notches and install support board C. Use clamps to hold it in place until the glue dries. Don't use any nails or screws on this joint, because the door-opening cut will be made through this board.

STEP 7 The front and back panels D are ¼"-thick veneer plywood that matches the solid wood. Cut them to the size listed in the materials list and attach them to the box, using glue and ¾"-long brass screws. Start the screws 1½" from each corner and space them about 5" to 6" apart.

STEP 8 To cut the box apart, set the angle of your table saw blade to 45°. The cut will be made through the support board C beginning 2¾" from the bottom of the box. The angle is toward the box top. The cut depth (or length) depends on the amount of rise on your blade. My cut is 1¾" deep, measured from the front of the toolbox. The blade should have a ⅛"-wide kerf (blade thickness) to remove enough material for the dust gasket. Push the box through the saw blade.

STEP 9 Extend the inner and outer angle cut lines, using a pencil and carpenter's square, to the box top. Set the table saw blade back to 90° and raise it above the table- top as high as possible. Carefully align the saw fence so the box will be guided through the blade between the pencil lines on each side of the the angle cut. Push the box through the saw blade.

STEP 10 Place ⅛"-thick spacers in the top saw kerf and clamp the door. Use two more clamps to secure the toolbox to your workbench. Verify that both saw cuts on each side are accurately joined with pencil lines. Use a sharp handsaw to complete the door cut between the two table saw cuts on each side. The table saw blade kerf will be thicker than a handsaw kerf, so a little sanding will be required to smooth both cuts.

STEP 11 Install a few more ¾"-long brass screws above and below the front face cut to further secure the front D to the support board.

STEP 12 Cut all the drawer parts to the sizes given in the materials list. The drawer box is 9" deep by 28½" wide by 3" high. Use a dado or standard blade on the table saw to form a ⅜"-deep by ¾"-wide rabbet cut on the back face at each end of the drawer front E.

STEP 13 The two drawer sides F and front E need a ¼"-wide by ⅜"-deep groove on the inside face to receive the bottom H. This groove begins ¼" above the bottom edge of each board.

STEP 14 Apply glue to the front board's rabbets and attach the sides with 1"-long brass screws. The grooves on the sides and front must align to receive the bottom board.

STEP 15 The drawer back G is 2½" high, so the ¼"-thick bottom H can be attached to its bottom edge. Attach the back G to the ends of the sides F with glue and 1½"-long screws. Slide the bottom panel into the grooves and secure it in place with a few brad nails driven into the back G.

STEP 16 The drawer support strips J are small strips of wood that are glued and screwed to the toolbox sides. Place the drawer box in the toolbox to locate and install these supports.

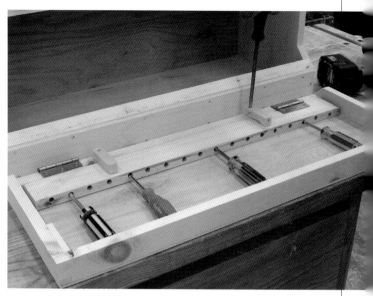

STEP 17 Attach the drawer stops K with glue and ¾" brass screws. They are located at the top of the door and in line with the drawer box. They will keep the drawer box closed when the toolbox door is closed.

STEP 18 The tool holder is optional, but it's a great addition to this box. The hole diameter in the rack should be sized for the type of tools that will be stored. Mine will be used for screwdrivers of all sizes, so I've drilled a series of ⅜"-diameter holes. The tool rack L is held in place by two small butt hinges. It's held tight to the door with wood locking blocks M that can be turned to lock or release the rack. However, don't install the rack, hinges, locking blocks or any other hardware at this point, because it's an ideal time to apply a finish to the toolbox. I'm using three coats of polyurethane to protect my toolbox.

STEP 19 Following the finish application, install feet so the box bottom won't be in contact with the floor. I'm using small rubber feet that are attached with ¾"screws and are available at most hardware stores.

STEP 20 The door is attached to the toolbox using a 30"-long by ½"-wide piano hinge. Note that you can only use ½"-long screws to secure the door part of the hinge, as longer screws will break through the front panel. Align the door face to the box front panel and the top to the toolbox top board. There should be a constant ⅛"-wide gap between the toolbox case and door.

STEP 21 Attach the tool rack using small butt hinges. The wood locking blocks can also be attached using 1¼"-long screws.

STEP 22 Each side of the toolbox will have a chest handle installed that's 3½" below the top surface of the box. I've used ¾"-long screws to attach my handles, but I suggest you use through-bolts and nuts if you plan to carry a lot of tools. You can also purchase larger chest handles, which are more comfortable, if they will be the primary method used to lift the toolbox.

STEP 23 A luggage handle can be installed on the top center of the toolbox for one-handed carrying. Use through-bolts with nuts instead of screws, because this handle will carry the total weight.

STEP 24 The drawer back G must be notched to clear the nuts on the luggage handle. Use a handsaw and chisel to cut the notches.

Building a Finger-Joint Jig

STEP 1 Attach a long 1" x 2" extension on your table saw miter fence. It will be used to support the finger-joint indexing panel.

STEP 2 Clamp an indexing panel, which is about 8" high and 24" long, to the extension board on your miter fence. This tall indexing panel will help support large boards as they are pushed through the dado blade. Once secured, cut through the indexing panel. I am setting up and testing this jig with a ½"-wide dado blade.

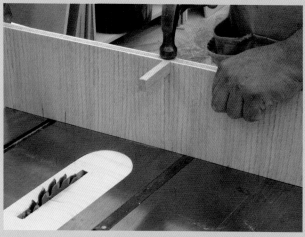

STEP 3 Cut a wood indexing pin, which equals the cut width, and glue it in the notch on the panel.

STEP 4 Use a loose indexing pin, which also is the same width as the notch, to set the fixed indexing pin ½" away from the dado blade. Clamp the indexing board securely to the miter fence extension.

STEP 5 Cut the two boards to be joined together. Hold the rear board tightly to the fixed indexing pin, and set the front board away from the fixed pin, using the loose indexing pin as a guide. Remove the loose indexing pin and make the first cut.

STEP 6 The second cut is made with the rear board notch over the indexing pin and the front board tight to the pin. Make the remaining cuts by moving the notches over the pin until all fingers and slots have been formed. If the test joint is loose, move the indexing panel so the fixed pin is slightly farther away from the blade. If the fingers are too wide for the notches, move the fixed indexing pin toward the blade. Be careful when moving the index board, because it doesn't take very much pin movement to dramatically change the finger and slot width.

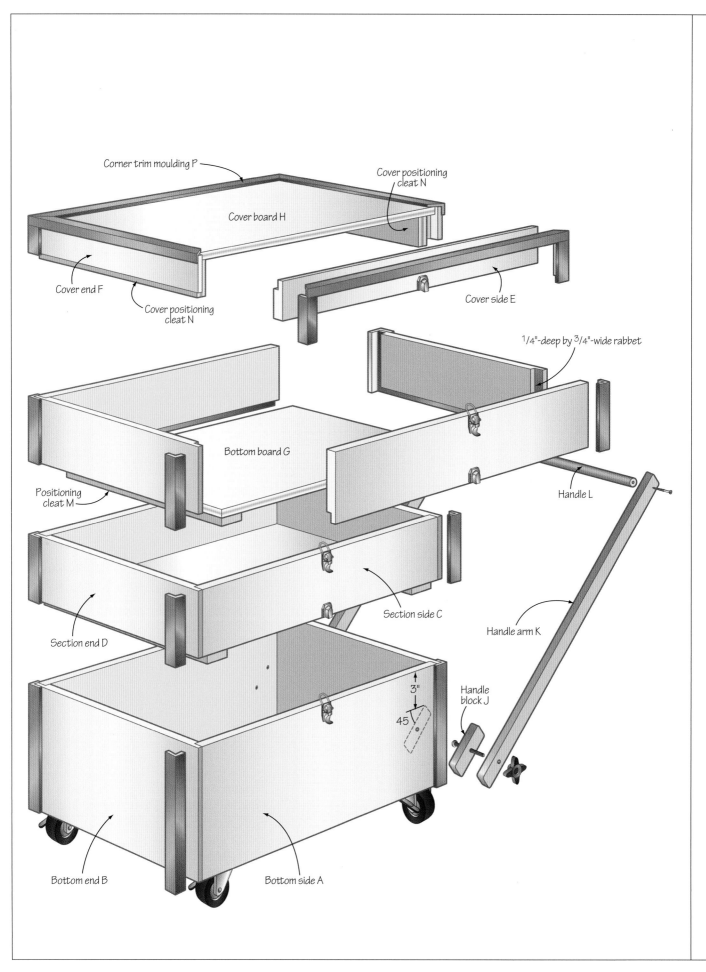

Corner trim moulding P

Cover positioning cleat N

Cover board H

Cover end F

Cover positioning cleat N

Cover side E

1/4"-deep by 3/4"-wide rabbet

Bottom board G

Positioning cleat M

Handle L

Section end D

Section side C

Handle arm K

3"

Handle block J

45

Bottom end B

Bottom side A

STEP 25 The gasket I'm using is called heavy-duty foam tape weatherstripping and is available in hardware stores. This material is commonly used to weather-strip doors and is self-adhesive and waterproof. The size that seems to work best is ³⁄₁₆" thick by ¾" wide. The tape will form a gasket that should keep most of the dirt and sawdust from entering the toolbox.

STEP 26 The final step is to install two draw catches to hold the door closed. Use ¾"-long screws and space the catches evenly on the box. You can also add a lock at this point if you need added security for your toolbox.

CONSTRUCTION
notes

So many options and changes can be made when designing your toolbox. The first choice, as mentioned at the start of this project, relates to the type of wood used. Hardwood will machine better, and you will have less tear-out on the fingers and slots compared to softwood. However, softwood is less expensive, lighter and easier to cut, but be aware of the results.

The tool rack can be customized to hold a lot of different tools. You might find it more useful to store marking tools or chisels in the rack, so drill and space the holes to suit your needs. Alternately, you might find the door space more valuable for tools like levels and squares, which means you'll need to design another style of holder.

Hardware is a major part of this project. If you plan to move this toolbox a great deal, or use it on a job site every day, you should purchase heavy-duty chest handles, draw catches and luggage handles. Use through-bolts and nuts in place of screws when attaching the heavier hardware. The chest handles I've used are more decorative than practical, and I wouldn't want to be lifting the box using these handles on a daily basis. I did see large, comfortable, industrial-style chest handles that would be much better suited for everyday use.

This toolbox has one 3"-high drawer but can have two 2"-high drawers or any combination of sizes. Look at what you plan to carry in your toolbox and decide which drawer design is best suited to your needs.

I built a couple of boxes using a special, thin-kerf blade, so the door gap was almost eliminated. That's another option you may want, but I like the gasket feature, which should help to eliminate the dust and dirt that builds up in toolboxes.

Before you begin to build this toolbox, decide on the best overall size for your needs. It can be made larger or smaller with a few minor dimensional changes. If you need to carry large tools, such as framing squares, the box will have to be taller. The plans are flexible and can be altered to meet your needs.

Carver's Tool Chest

I've always been interested in woodcarving, but haven't had the time or equipment to get started. This dedicated carver's tool chest is my way of getting motivated. Now that I have a special place for carving tools, I can begin putting everything together.

Those of you who carve wood know that a clean, well-organized storage cabinet is an important requirement. Dozens of knives, chisels, mallets and other tools must be within easy reach and kept in an area intended to protect the finely ground edges. It's not very productive, and often frustrating, when you have to spend valuable time looking for the right carving tool.

This chest is constructed using solid hardwood, with the exception of the top shelf, back and tray bottom boards. It has two 2"-high trays and two that are 3" high. The hinged top covers another storage compartment, so there should be enough room to meet most carvers' needs. The shallow, wide trays, as well as the upper compartment, will let you separate tools so they are easily seen and accessible.

There are hundreds of ways to build a tool chest; this project demonstrates one method. The top lid and side center panels are glued-up solid boards. I'll detail an easy way to make raised panels on a table saw so you won't need an expensive router or shaper to build this chest.

The trays glide on wooden runners, which was a common technique before modern hardware was available. The trays have solid-wood backs, fronts and sides, with grooves that allow them to travel along the wood glides. And because most carving tools are small and light, a simple veneer plywood drawer bottom is all that's needed.

Dedicated carvers will appreciate the features built into this chest. However, if you're like me and want to get started in carving, building this chest is a great beginning. I enjoyed building this project, and I'm sure you will as well.

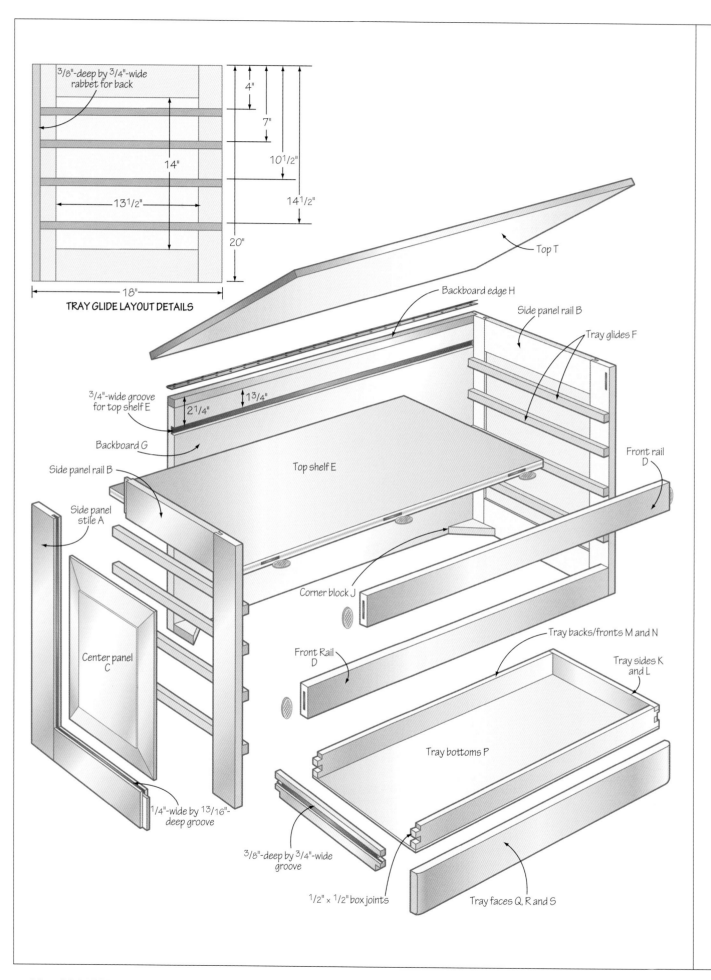

TRAY GLIDE LAYOUT DETAILS

3/8"-deep by 3/4"-wide rabbet for back

4"

7"

10 1/2"

14 1/2"

14"

13 1/2"

20"

18"

Top T

Backboard edge H

Side panel rail B

Tray glides F

3/4"-wide groove for top shelf E

2 1/4"

1 3/4"

Backboard G

Front rail D

Side panel rail B

Top shelf E

Side panel stile A

Corner block J

Center panel C

Front Rail D

Tray backs/fronts M and N

Tray sides K and L

Tray bottoms P

1/4"-wide by 13/16"-deep groove

3/8"-deep by 3/4"-wide groove

1/2" × 1/2" box joints

Tray faces Q, R and S

Schedule of Materials: Carver's Tool Chest

LTR.	NO.	ITEM	STOCK	INCHES T	(MM) T	INCHES W	(MM) W	INCHES L	(MM) L
A	4	side panel stiles	hardwood	¾	(19)	2¼	(57)	20	(508)
B	4	side panel rails	hardwood	¾	(19)	3	(76)	15	(381)
C	2	center panels	hardwood	¾	(19)	15	(381)	15½	(394)
D	2	front rails	hardwood	¾	(19)	3	(76)	28	(711)
E	1	top shelf	veneer ply	¾	(19)	16⅞	(429)	28	(711)
F	8	tray glides	hardwood	⅜	(10)	¹¹⁄₁₆	(18)	17	(432)
G	1	back board	veneer ply	¾	(19)	19½	(495)	28¾	(730)
H	1	back board edge	hardwood	¾	(19)	½	(13)	28¾	(730)
J	4	corner blocks	hardwood	¾	(19)	3½	(89)	3½	(89)
K	4	upper tray sides	hardwood	¾	(19)	2	(51)	17	(432)
L	4	lower tray sides	hardwood	¾	(19)	3	(76)	17	(432)
M	4	upper backs and fronts	hardwood	¾	(19)	2	(51)	27¹⁵⁄₁₆	(710)
N	4	lower backs and fronts	hardwood	¾	(19)	3	(76)	27¹⁵⁄₁₆	(710)
P	4	tray bottoms	veneer ply	¼	(6)	17	(432)	27¹⁵⁄₁₆	(710)
Q	2	top tray faces	hardwood	¾	(19)	3¼	(83)	29½	(749)
R	1	middle tray face	hardwood	¾	(19)	4	(102)	29½	(749)
S	1	bottom tray face	hardwood	¾	(19)	4½	(114)	29½	(749)
T	1	top	hardwood	¾	(19)	19	(483)	31½	(800)

Supplies

Glue

No. 10 Biscuits

Brad nails

¾" (19mm) Screws

1¼" (32mm) Screws

1   29½" (749mm) Piano hinge

2   12" (305mm) Lid chains

8   Tray handles

STEP ONE Before you begin, glue up the solid-wood side center panels C and wood top T. They require time for the adhesive to set, so after joining and clamping, put them aside until needed. As discussed in project ten, you don't need a jointer to successfully glue up solid wood. Ask the lumberyard to prepare the boards, which many will do for a small fee. However, a well-tuned table saw with a sharp blade will cut edges that are acceptable for this type of joinery. Be sure your saw fence is parallel to the saw blade and the blade is sharp. Cut one edge of the board, then flip it over so the cut edge is against the fence and cut the opposite side. Try to maintain an even, steady speed when feeding the boards through the saw blade, removing small amounts on each pass. You may have to repeat this step one or two times, but you will get edges that can be joined. If you prefer, edge joinery can be successfully done using a hand plane specifically made to plane edges. A good plane can be a real asset to your solid-panel work, and it's a worthwhile investment. If you haven't got room for a power jointer, or don't appreciate the noise it generates, consider purchasing a hand plane. Edge-join the top panel T using glue and biscuits. However, the two center panels C must be edge-joined using only glue, because a lot of wood will be removed when the panels are raised, and a biscuit joint may be exposed.

STEP 2 Cut the side panel stiles A and rails B to the sizes indicated in the materials list. Use a table saw to form a ¼"-wide by ¹³⁄₁₆"-deep groove along one edge of each piece. To ensure the groove is centered on your ¾" stock, set the inside face of the saw blade ¼" away from the fence. Push the boards through the blade, then reverse the board and run it through the blade again. That process will center the groove, but a small strip of material may be left in the middle if your blade is less than ⅛" thick. If that's the case, adjust the fence and run a cleaning pass in the center of each groove.

STEP 3 Each of the four rails B requires a ¼"-thick by ¾"-long tenon on both ends. These can be cut with a standard saw blade by making multiple passes over the blade or with a dado blade. Test the cuts on scrap material to be sure the tenons fit properly in the grooves.

STEP 4 Cut the two side center panels C to size. These panels will be raised on a table saw. First, lower the blade below the table surface and secure a strong board across its center 90° to the blade face. The best blade for this technique is a large-kerf (thick) rip blade. The miter slide can be used to align the guide board.

STEP 5 Begin with the blade ¹⁄₃₂" above the table surface. Push all four sides of both center panels along the guide board and across the blade. Repeat the process, raising the blade ¹⁄₃₂" after each series of passes, until the edges of the panels fit loosely into the stile and rail grooves. Be sure the panels can move freely inside the grooves to allow for expansion and contraction of the wood. Slow, steady passes across the blade will yield the best cuts and reduce sanding after the cuts have been completed. Use a push pad in the center of each panel so the panel won't tip as the edges get thinner.

STEP 6 Sand the panel edges and assemble both side panels, using glue on the tenons only. Clamp them securely until the glue sets up. The center panels should float in the grooves. Ensure the frames are square by measuring the diagonals. If the dimensions are the same, the panel is square.

STEP 7 Form a ¾"-wide by ⅜"-deep rabbet on the rear inside face of each side panel. Use a dado blade on your table saw or a router with a ¾" straight-cutting bit along with a guide.

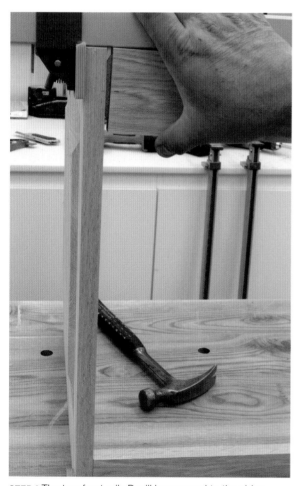

STEP 9 The top compartment's fixed shelf E is 16⅞" deep. It will extend ⅜" into the space for the rear rabbet cuts because it will be secured in a ⅜"-deep groove on the backboard G. The bottom edge of this fixed shelf should be aligned with the bottom edge of the top rail. Turn the cabinet on its top edges and mark the position for three biscuit slots on the bottom face. Cut the slots in both top shelf E and upper front rail D. Check the fit, then take the case apart.

STEP 8 The two front rails D will be secured to the sides using biscuit joinery. Use No. 10 biscuits for this application because the No. 20 is too wide. Cut a biscuit slot on the center ends of each rail, and a slot in the side panels. The top rail is flush with the top edges of the side panels, and the bottom is flush with the lower ends. Once you have cut the biscuit slots, dry fit the parts but do not glue them at this point.

STEP 10 The tray glides F are hardwood strips. They can be installed at this point, before assembling the case, using glue and a ¾"-long screw at each end. The strips are attached at points measured from the top edge of each side panel. The positions, from the side edge top surface to the top edge of each glide, are 4", 7", 10½" and 14½".

STEP 11 The case can now be assembled using glue on the biscuits and along both sides of the top shelf E. This shelf will be held more securely once its back edge is placed in the backboard's groove. When all the parts are properly aligned, clamp the case and wait until the adhesive cures.

STEP 12 The backboard is 20" high and is a combination of the back board edge strip H attached to the ¾"-thick panel of veneer plywood G. Attach the hardwood strip to the top edge, using glue and brad nails. Cut a ¾"-wide by ⅜"-deep groove in the backboard to receive the top shelf E. The groove's top edge is 2¼" below the top edge of the backboard with the hardwood strip in place. Put glue in the groove and on the rabbet cuts on each side panel. Install the backboard with the hardwood strip on the top edge and the fixed shelf E in the groove. Clamp the assembly or drive a few brad nails through the back face of the backboard to keep it secure.

STEP 13 Strengthen the bottom section of the case by installing four corner blocks J. Cut them on a 45° angle to size and attach them using glue and brad nails.

STEP 14 The trays are ¹⁄₁₆" narrower than the cabinet's inside width. The sides, back and front boards are ¾" hardwood stock. I will detail the process used to make box joints for the corner joinery, but many other joints can be used. If you do decide to use a screw and butt joint, don't place the screws in the middle of the side boards, because grooves will be cut in the center. Cut parts K, L, M and N to size, then set up your ½" box-cutting jig (see the sidebar "Building a Finger-Joint Jig" at the end of project ten). These are narrow boards, so use a square to make certain they are aligned 90° to the table saw top before cutting.

STEP 15 Each finger and slot for these box joints is ½" wide. To properly interlock, the sides K and L are indexed differently than the fronts and backs M and N. Use the indexing pin to space the sides ½" away from the fixed pin on each initial cut. The backs and fronts can be started tight to the fixed pin. That setup will align the fingers and notches correctly. Remember to orient the boards properly when cutting each end. To guarantee correct positioning, place a mark on the bottom edges of the 16 tray boards. Now, start all the cuts on both ends of each board with the mark facing the fixed pin.

STEP 16 Assemble the four trays with glue applied to all fingers and slots. Clamp the trays and measure the diagonals to ensure they are square. If the measurements are different, a slight twist or tap on the long side will equalize the measurements.

STEP 17 I want as much depth as possible in each tray. To achieve this, I'm using ¼"-thick veneer plywood for the tray bottoms P. Nail and glue the tray bottoms P to the tray frame bottoms.

STEP 19 The tray faces Q, R and S are the full cabinet width at 29½". Cut all four faces to the sizes indicated in the materials list and round over each front outside face with a ⅜"-radius roundover bit.

STEP 18 A ¾"-wide groove is needed on both sides of each tray. They will fit over the tray glides F and should be centered on each side. If the cutting, assembly and measurements are correct, the grooves should all be ⅜" deep. However, that's not always the case, so I suggest you sneak up on the correct groove depth. The best tool to cut these grooves is a stacked dado blade on a table saw. Begin with a ¼"-deep groove on each side and test fit the tray. If necessary, cut the grooves a little deeper to achieve the correct fit. The tray should be snug on the glides, without binding, because they will be fine-tuned and waxed after finishing until they slide smoothly.

STEP 20 Attach the tray faces to the tray boxes using three 1¼"-long screws through the back side of the front boards. The easiest way to properly align the faces is to first drill the handle holes in the tray faces only. Then, using a 2½"-high spacer under the bottom face, drive screws through the handle holes into the tray box. Now that the face is securely attached to the tray box in the correct position, it can be slid open to install the 1¼" screws inside the tray. Remove the front screws and install the handles after completing the handle-hole drilling. Continue the installation process, moving up one face at a time with a ¹⁄₁₆"-thick spacer between tray faces.

STEP 21 The top T is a glued-up hardwood panel. It's installed flush with the backboard and extends 1" past the front and sides of the chest. Cut it to size and round over the top and bottom edges of the sides with a ⅜"-radius bit in a router. Leave the bottom, back edge square so there will be a straight edge to install the piano hinge. Mount the top with a 29½"-long by ½"-wide piano hinge. Set the nails that hold the wood edge strip on top of the backboard ¼" below the surface with a nail set punch. The hinge recess can be cut on the table saw by setting your blade ½" above the tabletop, and the fence-to-blade distance ⅛" smaller than the chest height.

STEP 22 Attach two 12"-long chains to the chest lid to limit its travel. Once the trays and lid are operating correctly, apply a finish.

CONSTRUCTION
notes

Many of my wood projects are built using red oak, and this one is no exception. However, any hardwood, or softwood for that matter, that's reasonably priced in your area can be used.

The most important design issue is the tray size, and the options are endless. Inventory the tools you want to store and change the tray sizes to suit your requirements. Also, the trays can be lined with felt to protect delicate carving knives or equipped with holders so your chisels and knives have a dedicated space.

This is a large tool chest, which may be sized correctly for many carvers, but it can be easily made smaller or larger if needed. The top can also be fitted with a lock if you want to secure expensive, and potentially dangerous, knives and fine carving tools. The trays may be a little more difficult to outfit with locks, with the exception of the top tray, which could easily be secured using the top rail.

When I researched this project, I came across many carving chests that did have tool holders. They were the half-circle type and typically held chisels. I didn't want to design the insert holders until I had all my carving tools because there are so many types and styles of handles on the market. I believe these holders should be customized for your tools, so that part of the project will be your design.

Finally, don't be intimidated by the box joints; you can use a number of other corner joints, like simple butt joints to build the trays. Remember to keep any hardware outside the ¾"-wide groove path that must be cut in each side board. You can also use dovetail joints for the tray corners if you feel confident using that method. Remember to apply a good coat of hard paste wax to the drawer glides once in a while, and they will provide years of reliable service.

Mobile Tool Chest

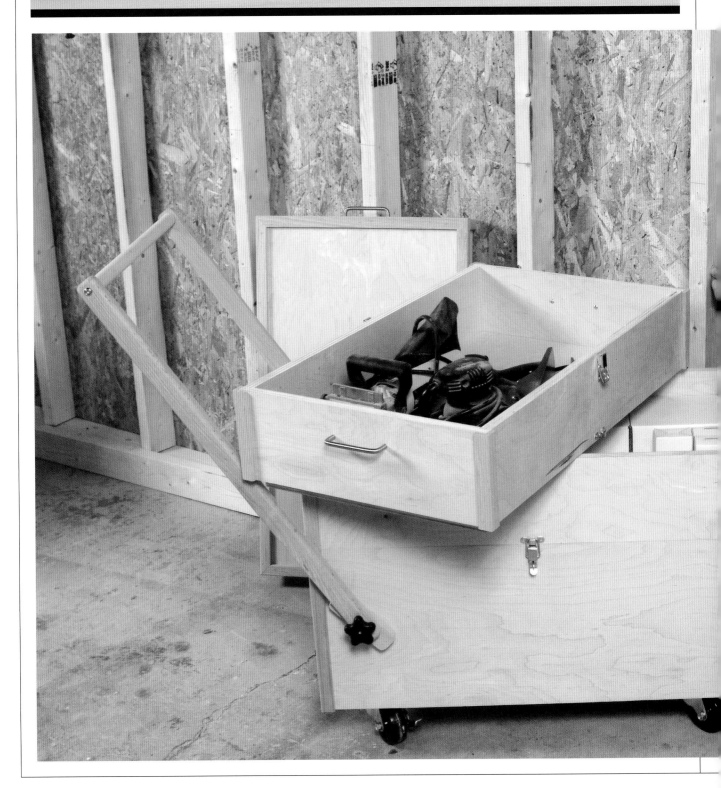

How do you build a mobile toolbox to suit everyone's needs? That's the question I faced when designing this project. I soon realized that I couldn't meet everyone's requirements. A woodworker who likes building deck and outdoor projects has very different tool storage requirements than someone who does a lot of interior trim carpentry.

I decided to make a sectional mobile chest that could be broken down and loaded in a car, truck or van. The sections can be any height and divided based on the types of tools and hardware required. The basic chest design is built the same no matter what your needs are; only the interior divisions are customized.

I designed the pull handle so it could swing over the lower (main) section for storage or transportation. Each box can be stacked on any other box, and you can assemble any combination of boxes to take along to the work site. The cover fits and latches to any section, so any combination of boxes that you decide to carry will have a latched top.

The ability to carry one section at a time is a real bonus. For years I've been lifting heavy tool chests into my vehicles, and my back has suffered the consequences. I don't know why I hadn't thought of the sectional tool chest concept before this. It's such a simple idea!

My tools are organized in their own sections. The heavy electric tools such as drills, jigsaws and sanders are in the bottom box. Hand tools are stored in another smaller top section, and the last section is dedicated to my hardware supplies for the particular project I'm working on. When I get to the project site, I simply take the sections apart and I'm ready to work without having to dig through a deep chest to sort my tools.

If you need tools and hardware on a job site, or do a lot of projects for family and friends, or just want a safe, secure and organized tool storage area, this is the project for you. I'm sure you'll enjoy building the mobile chest and custom designing the sections.

Schedule of Materials: Mobile Tool Chest

LTR.	NO.	ITEM	STOCK	INCHES T	(MM) T	INCHES W	(MM) W	INCHES L	(MM) L
A	2	bottom sides	veneer ply	¾	(19)	12	(305)	29	(737)
B	2	bottom ends	veneer ply	¾	(19)	12	(305)	18	(457)
C	4	section sides	veneer ply	¾	(19)	6	(152)	29	(737)
D	4	section ends	veneer ply	¾	(19)	6	(152)	18	(457)
E	2	cover sides	veneer ply	¾	(19)	3	(76)	29	(737)
F	2	cover ends	veneer ply	¾	(19)	3	(76)	18	(457)
G	3	bottom boards	veneer ply	¾	(19)	17	(432)	29	(737)
H	1	cover board	veneer ply	¾	(19)	17	(432)	29	(737)
J	2	handle blocks	hardwood	¾	(19)	1½	(38)	5	(127)
K	2	handle arms	hardwood	¾	(19)	13⁹⁄₁₆	(344)	30	(762)
L	1	handle	wood dowel	1	(25)			20¼	(514)
M	4	positioning cleats	veneer ply	¾	(19)	2	(51)	16½	(419)
N	2	cover position cleats	veneer ply	¾	(19)	3	(76)	16½	(419)
P	1	corner trim moulding	hardwood	1	(25)	1	(25)	24	(7315)

Supplies

Note: Quantities will vary depending on the number of chest sections built.

Glue

Brad nails

1½" (38mm) Screws

1¼" (32mm) Screws

16 ¼" x 1½" (6mm x 38mm) Carriage bolts with nuts

2   ¼" x 2" (6mm x 51mm) Carriage bolts

2   Handle-locking knobs

4   Wheels/casters

8   Chest handles

6   Draw latches

2   Decorative finishing washers

STEP 1 Cut the section panels A, B, C, D, E and F to the sizes indicated in the materials list. These panel dimensions are based on my stackable section sizes of a 12"-high base unit and two 6"-high top sections, as well as a chest cover. If you've decided on a different size configuration, please change the sizes before cutting the sheet material. Each of the B, D and F end panels needs a ¾"-wide by ¼"-deep rabbet on each end to receive the side panels. Use a stacked carbide dado blade, or router equipped with a ¾" bit, to form the rabbets.

STEP 2 Leave the dado blade set in the same position as in step 1. Cut a ¾"-wide by ¼"-deep rabbet on the inside face (same face as the previous rabbets) of all sides and end panels. These rabbets will receive the bottom and cover panels.

STEP 3 Assemble the four frames by securing the sides in the end rabbets with glue and 1½"-long screws. Drill pilot holes for the screws to minimize material splits. The screw heads will be hidden by corner moulding. The rabbets on the long edges of the panels should be aligned to properly receive the bottom boards G.

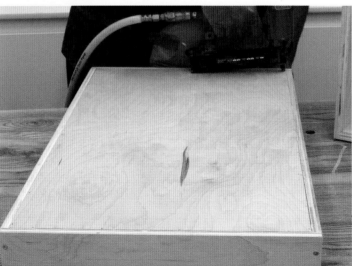

STEP 4 The bottom boards G and cover board H are installed in the frame rabbets. Use glue and a few brad nails, driven through the face side, to secure these panels.

STEP 5 Attach the two handle blocks J. These blocks will allow the handle arms K to clear the corner moulding, which will be attached in a later step. Before securing the blocks on the base case, drill holes in the center of each one and install a 2"-long by ¼"-diameter carriage bolt. You'll need to counterbore the bolt holes so the carriage bolt head is beneath the block surface. Use a sander to remove and round the handle block corners. The handle block will be installed at a 45° angle, 3" below the top edge and 1" in from the case end panel. Use glue and 1¼"-long screws, through the inside face of the bottom case sides, to attach the blocks.

STEP 6 Drill a ¹⁵⁄₁₆"-diameter hole on one end of each handle arm K. The holes should be 1¼" in from each end and centered on the handle. Use a ⅜"-radius roundover bit in your router to soften the outside edges of both handle arms. These arms will be attached to the handle blocks using ¼" threaded knobs, which are available at many home-improvement and hardware stores.

STEP 7 The handle L is a 1"-diameter wood dowel rod. Drill a ⅜"-deep by 1"-diameter hole on the inside face of each handle arm. Center the hole ¾" below the top end on each arm. Install the handle in the arm holes and secure each end with a 1¼"-long screw and decorative finishing washer. Don't use glue on these joints, as you may want to dismantle the handle and arm assembly in the future. The handle arms, with handle attached, should fold over the opposite end of the bottom case to minimize space when transporting the chest.

STEP 8 I'm installing 3"-diameter wheels, which have a locking option, on my toolbox base section. The wheel base plates are set 1½" in from each end edge. Use 1½"-long by ¼"-diameter carriage bolts to attach the wheels. My stackable toolbox will be used in my shop, on concrete floors in a garage or on paved driveways most of the time. However, if your chest will be used on rough or uneven surfaces, such as grass and unpaved driveways, you should consider installing larger-diameter wheels.

STEP 9 Cut the positioning cleats M to the size shown. They are aligned ¾" in from each section edge and secured with 1¼"-long screws. Don't glue these cleats, because not only do they align the sections when stacked, they also act as feet and may need replacing when worn.

STEP 10 The cover should also be fitted with the two positioning cleats N. Secure them to the inside face of each cover end panel using 1¼"-long screws. These cleats will position and align the cover on any of the stackable trays.

STEP 12 I'm installing simple metal D-handles on all sections as well as the cover. These are medium-duty handles, but you can just as easily install heavy-duty chest handles if you plan to carry heavier loads in your chest.

STEP 11 Attach draw latches on each stackable section. Be sure to align and secure each latch in the same position so any section, or cover, can be attached to different stack arrangements. This mix-and-match feature is handy, so take extra care when installing these latches.

STEP 13 The corner trim moulding P installed around the cover's top perimeter, as well as the trim on the chest section corners, is 1" corner moulding. This trim is available in all lumberyards. I'm using oak to contrast with the maple veneer, but any wood will be fine. If you plan to paint your chest, use inexpensive finger- jointed pine trim. Cut the pieces to size and attach them around the cover rim, as well as on the four vertical corners of each chest section, using glue and brad nails.

STEP 14 The interior spaces of each stackable section can be divided or left open based on your requirements. Customize the space in each section for tools and hardware.

CONSTRUCTION
notes

This mobile tool chest project has dozens of design options. I mentioned a few in the introduction and throughout the construction steps. However, the height, width and length of each stackable section are the most obvious changes that can be made.

You may not need 6"-deep stackables or a 12"-deep base. If that's the case, change the sizes to suit your needs. As previously mentioned, the width and type of terrain this unit will be pulled over will determine how wide and what style of wheels you should use. If you do a lot of deck building, I would suggest you widen the base and use large-diameter wheels for the rugged yards you'll most likely encounter.

I used ¾" maple veneer plywood and oak trim for my project. The chest is finished with three coats of water-based polyurethane. However, I was going to use plywood and finger-jointed pine trim. In that case, I would finish the chest with two or three coats of latex paint. But as I was walking through my local sheet material supplier, I noticed a few sheets of veneered maple seconds for sale. They were less expensive than the regular plywood, so I saved a few dollars and had a smoother surface to finish. That's one of the benefits with this project, because you can use any ¾"-thick plywood sheet material. So look around your area for a good buy on sheet stock.

Also as previously mentioned, consider the loads that will be carried in the chest sections. If you plan to carry heavy tools, use heavy-duty chest handles on the sections. Consider using 1½" x 1½" square boards for the handle arms and a 1¼"-diameter dowel rod if you will be pulling heavy loads over rough surfaces.

Simple Workbench

workbench in any woodshop is a necessary item. Most benches are the center of activity in the workroom and one of your most important tools. However, if you share your work space with the family car in the garage,or with the pool table in the basement activity room, or if you must work in the backyard, having a good sturdy bench isn't always possible.

How would you like a strong bench, with an accessory shelf, that can be assembled in minutes or taken apart just as quickly for storage? What about having all bench parts bolted together when stored so you'll be able to find everything quickly? This simple workbench project may be just what you need — sturdy, easy to put together, quick to take apart and suitable for any of your woodworking projects.

This simple workbench can be built for less than $80, using one ¾"-thick sheet of plywood, a half sheet of hardboard, a few feet of hardwood for the table-top trim and three 8' lengths of framing lumber. It's extremely sturdy and can be built in one evening in your workshop with a few simple electric tools. In fact, if your local lumberyard can cut the plywood sheet to size, half the work will be done.

I've built this bench with hardware so the shelf and leg assemblies can be easily taken apart. But you can use glue and screws, as I will detail in the construction notes, if you don't need to take the bench apart. The top is 1¾" thick, perfectly flat and strong enough to hold any project in progress.

The fold-flat storage feature is important to many woodworkers who share their work space, but a contractor friend of mine mentioned another use that I hadn't considered. He is going to build the bench and use it for on-site work where a strong worktable is a real bonus. He also said this bench design would be handy for any woodworker who helps family and friends with their renovation projects. Maybe this should be called the traveling workbench project.

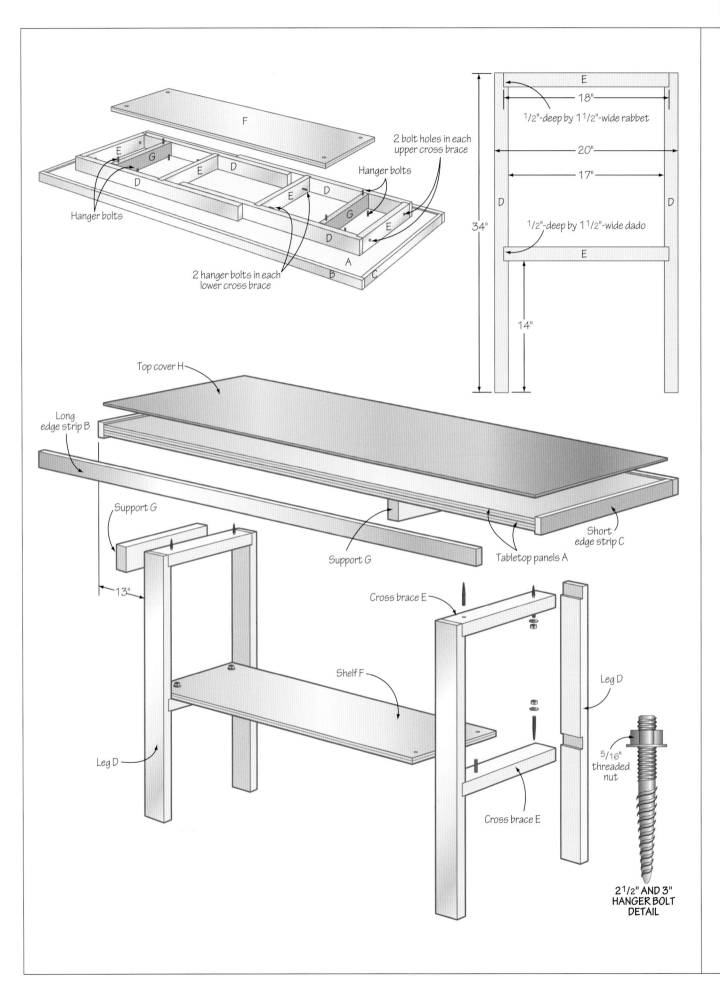

F

E

G

E D

D

Hanger bolts

2 bolt holes in each
upper cross brace

Hanger bolts

E

D

G

E

2 hanger bolts in each
lower cross brace

A

B

C

E

18"

1/2"-deep by 1 1/2"-wide rabbet

20"

17"

D

D

34"

1/2"-deep by 1 1/2"-wide dado

E

14"

Top cover H

Long
edge strip B

Support G

Support G

Tabletop panels A

Short
edge strip C

13"

Cross brace E

Shelf F

Leg D

Leg D

5/16"
threaded
nut

Leg D

Cross brace E

2 1/2" AND 3"
HANGER BOLT
DETAIL

Schedule of Materials: Simple Workbench

LTR.	NO.	ITEM	STOCK	INCHES T	(MM) T	INCHES W	(MM) W	INCHES L	(MM) L
A	2	tabletop panels	plywood	¾	(19)	23¹⁵⁄₁₆	(608)	72	(1829)
B	2	long edge strips	hardwood	¾	(19)	1¾	(45)	73½	(1867)
C	2	short edge strips	hardwood	¾	(19)	1¾	(45)	23¹⁵⁄₁₆	(608)
D	4	legs	softwood	1½	(38)	3½	(89)	34	(864)
E	4	cross braces	softwood	1½	(38)	3½	(89)	18	(457)
F	1	shelf	plywood	¾	(19)	17	(432)	48	(1219)
G	2	supports	softwood	1½	(38)	3½	(89)	17	(432)
H	1	top cover	hardboard	¼	(6)	23¹⁵⁄₁₆	(608)	72	(1829)

Supplies

Nails

Glue

2" (51mm) Screws

8   ⁵⁄₁₆" x 2½" (8mm x 64mm) Hanger bolts

4   ⁵⁄₁₆" x 3" (8mm x 76mm) Hanger bolts

12 ⁵⁄₁₆" (8mm) Washers

12 ⁵⁄₁₆" (8mm) Nuts

STEP 1 Prepare the two tabletop plywood panels A for the workbench top. The first cut, to optimize the 4' x 8' sheet, should be a crosscut along the width so you'll have one panel at 48" x 72" and one shorter panel at 48" wide. The shorter panel will be used for the bench shelf later in the project. Rip the longer panel into two equal sheets that are approximately 23⁵⁄₁₆" wide by 72" long. The kerf (thickness) of your blade will determine the final width after cutting the sheets; however, most blades are about ⅛" thick. If you don't have a table saw capable of cutting the large panels, use a circular saw or have the lumberyard cut the panels to size.

STEP 2 Use glue to bond the two sheets together, creating a top that's 1½" thick by 23¹⁵⁄₁₆" wide by 72" long. Hold the sheets in alignment with a few small nails and place weight on the panel until the adhesive sets.

SHOP tip

If you don't own a router table or dado blade set for your table saw, you can make rabbets and dadoes with a circular saw. Draw cut lines on the lumber, set the saw blade depth to ½", and make a series of kerf cuts within the lines for each rabbet or dado. Break the small pieces with a chisel and hammer, then clean the joint with a sharp chisel.

STEP 3 The workbench top will have a cover made of hardboard, sometimes called Masonite, that's available in a number of thicknesses. Measure the thickness of the sandwiched plywood panel and the hardboard cover. I'm using ¼" hardboard for my cover, so the total top thickness is 1¾". Cut the two long edge strips B and two short edge strips C to the sizes indicated in the materials list, or to the correct size for your table if your top dimensions are different from mine. Mount the strips flush with the bottom face of the plywood panel so they will be ¼" above the top surface. This lip rising above the surface will hold the hardboard cover in place. Secure the edge strips with glue and 2" screws (or biscuit joinery if you have the tools and want to hide the edge fasteners). Small finishing nails and glue can also be used to hold the strips. The joinery technique doesn't matter as long as you are satisfied with the appearance.

STEP 4 The leg assemblies are made with 2x4 framing lumber. Cut parts D and E to the lengths stated and form the dadoes and rabbets on the four legs D. All dadoes and rabbets are ½" deep by 1½" wide and located as shown in the illustration.

STEP 5 Build the two leg assemblies by first putting glue in the rabbets and dadoes. Join the cross braces E and legs D as shown and drive 2" screws in pilot holes through the leg into each cross brace. Two screws per joint, along with the glue, will create a strong bond. Remember to drill pilot holes for the screws to avoid splitting the soft lumber.

STEP 6 Draw position lines across the underside of the table-top that are 13" from each end. Measure and draw cross lines (about 2¹¹⁄₁₆") from each table side to position each leg assembly on the center of the workbench top.

STEP 7 Position the leg assemblies and drill two ³⁄₁₆"-diameter holes through each upper brace into the workbench top. Drill 1" into the plywood panels. Set the leg assemblies aside, then in the workbench top, thread the coarse end of a 3"-long by ⁵⁄₁₆"-diameter hanger bolt into each hole, leaving 2" of the bolt exposed. Enlarge the through-holes in both braces so the leg assemblies will fit over the shafts of the ⁵⁄₁₆" bolts . Secure the legs with washers and nuts.

SHOP tip

Many woodworking stores carry a large selection of threaded hanger bolts and knobs. You can use these knobs in place of the nuts for quicker assembly.

STEP 8 Once both leg assemblies have been securely fastened, turn the workbench right-side up. Cut the shelf F to size using the offcut from the plywood sheet. Drill two $3/16$"-diameter holes through each end of the shelf into the lower braces. Drill $1\frac{1}{4}$" into each brace. Secure the shelf panel to the lower braces using $5/16$" by $2\frac{1}{2}$"-long hanger bolts, washers and nuts.

STEP 9 If your bench will be used in a fixed position all the time (see the construction notes), proceed to step 11. Otherwise, remove the shelf and leg assemblies that are attached to the workbench top. Lay the legs on the bottom face of the top as shown. Next, cut two 17" lengths of 2x4s to create the supports G. Align the supports on the bench top so that the existing mounting holes in the shelf can be centered on each support, but be sure the supports don't cover the areas where the leg assemblies get attached to the bench top. Secure the supports with glue and two 2" screws driven through the top side of the workbench.

STEP 10 Use the shelf as a template to position hanger bolts in each support. Install ⁵⁄₁₆"-diameter by 2½"-long hanger bolts in each support. Put the shelf on the supports, with the legs lying flat, and secure the shelf board to the supports with nuts and washers. Tighten the nuts and test the folded-up position of your workbench.

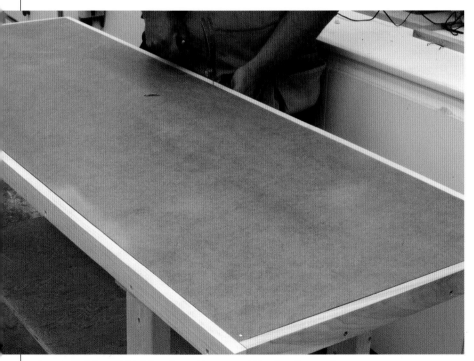

STEP 11 Cut the ¼"-thick hardboard top cover H to size. Secure the cover with a few small nails. These nails can be easily removed if the top needs replacing.

CONSTRUCTION
notes

The first decision you should make before building the workbench concerns its use. Do you want it assembled all the time? Will you use the fold-up feature? If you don't need to store the bench flat, replace the hanger bolts and nuts with glue and 2" screws to permanently secure the legs and shelf.

However, having the option to pack the bench flat could be a valuable asset if it needs to be transported for a move or taken to a work site. If you live in temporary quarters, share your woodworking space with the family car or work at woodworking projects only occasionally, the storage option might be worth considering.

I built the bench using ¼" G1S (good one side) plywood and construction-grade 2x4 lumber. You could use a less expensive sheet material like ¾" medium-density fiberboard (MDF) or particleboard to lower the cost. The legs could be made from hardwood, which is a little more resistant to damage, but that's a lot more costly than construction-grade softwood. The edge around the workbench top should be a hardwood, as that area will suffer a lot of bumps and scrapes. If you want to keep the cost as low as possible because you use the bench only three or four times each year, build it with construction-grade lumber and MDF sheet stock.

The bench can be protected with good oil-based paint. And if the floor in your work space is uneven, install adjustable feet or levelers on each leg. Adjustable feet are available at hardware stores and are usually installed in drilled holes in the leg bottoms. They provide about ¾" adjustment, which should be sufficient for most garage floors.

The Practical Workbench

I'm sure there are one hundred ways to build a workbench, and all of them are correct if they meet your needs. Here's a workbench that fills all my requirements and one that will hopefully be useful in your workshop.

A bench doesn't have to be pretty. A good hardwood that's straight and flat, with a few blemishes, is just fine. After all, we're going to be pounding, clamping, dragging and abusing the top in the years to come. The bench should be strong and heavy enough to withstand a bit of pushing and pulling when we are working wood.

I used ash for my bench and tried to keep the best faces for my top surface. Even though I selected the wood carefully, I did have a few little checks and knots to fill. This wood wasn't a select grade, so I didn't expect perfection. Carefully sort through the lesser grades of lumber and pick the best pieces for your bench. It may not win a beauty contest, but the price will be a lot less than select-grade lumber.

A bench needs one or two good vises and, since a bench has a great deal of space below, a storage cabinet for frequently used tools. This bench has five drawers for tools and a shelf for tucking those tools aside when you are working on a project, keeping them within easy reach.

I installed two Veritas vises on my bench. The twin-screw model is a well-machined and very useful tool. The single-screw model mounted on the right side of the bench is perfect for my work. Both vises are available at Lee Valley Tools. The bench can be mounted on wheels, the vise styles and positions can be changed and the size can be altered for your shop. It's well worth your time and money to build a good workbench because it will be an important part of your shop for many years.

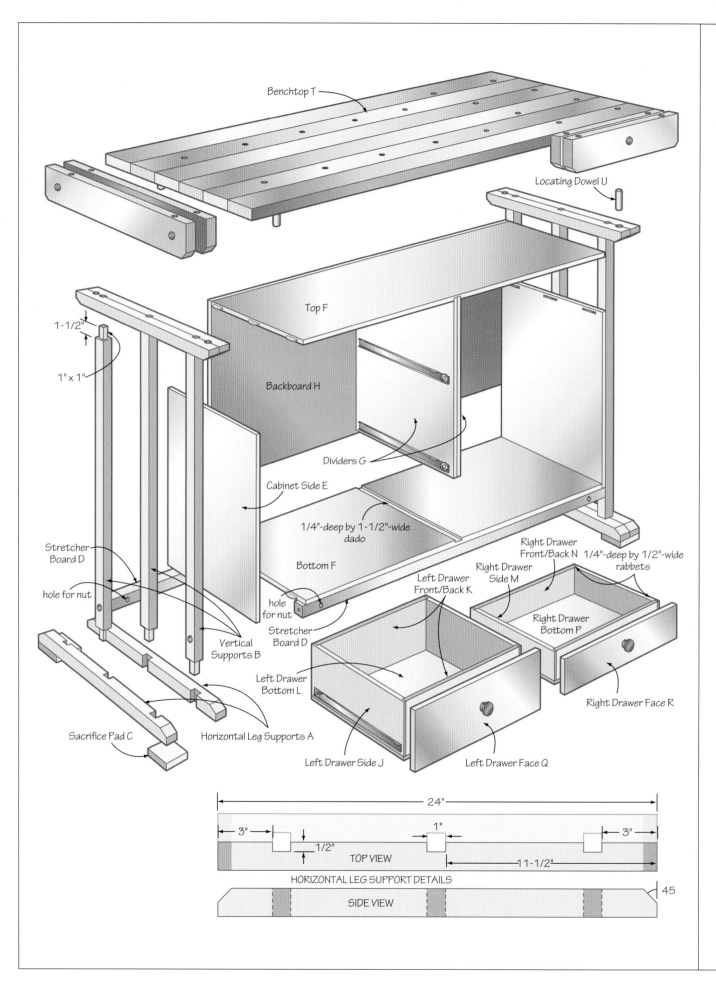

Benchtop T

Locating Dowel U

Top F

Backboard H

1-1/2"

1" x 1"

Dividers G

Cabinet Side E

1/4"-deep by 1-1/2"-wide dado

Right Drawer Front/Back N

1/4"-deep by 1/2"-wide rabbets

Right Drawer Side M

Bottom F

Left Drawer Front/Back K

Right Drawer Bottom P

Stretcher Board D

hole for nut

hole for nut

Stretcher Board D

Left Drawer Bottom L

Right Drawer Face R

Vertical Supports B

Sacrifice Pad C

Horizontal Leg Supports A

Left Drawer Side J

Left Drawer Face Q

24"

3"

1"

3"

1/2"

TOP VIEW

11-1/2"

HORIZONTAL LEG SUPPORT DETAILS

SIDE VIEW

45

Schedule of Materials: The Practical Workbench

LTR.	NO.	ITEM	STOCK	INCHES T	(MM) T	INCHES W	(MM) W	INCHES L	(MM) L
A	8	horizontal supports	solid hardwood	1½	(38)	1½	(38)	24	(610)
B	6	vertical supports	solid hardwood	1½	(38)	1½	(38)	33½	(851)
C	4	sacrifice pads	solid hardwood	1	(25)	3	(76)	3	(76)
D	2	stretcher boards	solid hardwood	1½	(38)	2½	(64)	44	(1118)
E	2	cabinet sides	veneer plywood	¾	(19)	16¾	(425)	20	(508)
F	2	bottom & top boards	veneer plywood	¾	(19)	16¾	(425)	42½	(1080)
G	2	dividers	veneer plywood	¾	(19)	16¾	(425)	19	(483)
H	1	backboard	veneer plywood	¾	(19)	20	(508)	44	(1118)
Two left-side drawer boxes									
J	4	sides	birch plywood	½	(13)	6¾	(171)	16	(406)
K	4	fronts & backs	birch plywood	½	(13)	6¾	(171)	19	(483)
L	2	bottoms	birch plywood	½	(13)	16	(406)	19½	(496)
Three right-side drawer boxes									
M	6	sides	birch plywood	½	(13)	3⅝	(92)	16	(406)
N	6	fronts & backs	birch plywood	½	(13)	3⅝	(92)	19	(483)
P	3	bottoms	birch plywood	½	(13)	16	(406)	19½	(496)
Drawer faces									
Q	2	faces	veneer plywood	¾	(19)	9¾	(248)	21½	(546)
R	2	faces	veneer plywood	¾	(19)	6¾	(171)	21½	(546)
S	1	faces	veneer plywood	¾	(19)	6	(152)	21½	(546)
Benchtop									
T	1	benchtop	solid hardwood	1½	(38)	30	(762)	72	(1825)
U	4	locating dowels	solid hardwood	(1" diameter by 2½" long)					

Supplies - inches

5 Sets of 18"-long, ¾-extension glides (use full-extension glides if desired)

Drawer handles or knobs

PB screws

Bolts, nuts and washers as detailed

Plate joinery biscuits (#20)

Glue

4" x ⅜"-Diameter bolts with washers and nuts

Wood edge tape

1½" PB screws

1" Brad nails

½" Screws

1" Screws

Optional

1 Front vise (Veritas Tools by Lee Valley Tools #70G08.02)

1 Twin-screw vise (Veritas Tools by Lee Valley Tools #05G12.22)

4 Bench dogs (Veritas Tools by Lee Valley Tools #05G04.04)

Supplies - metric

5 Sets of 457mm-long, ¾-extension glides (use full-extension glides if desired)

Drawer handles or knobs

PB screws

Bolts, nuts and washers as detailed

Plate joinery biscuits (#20)

Glue

102mm × 10mm-diameter Bolts with washers and nuts

Wood edge tape

38mm PB screws

25mm Brad nails

13mm Screws

25mm Screws

Optional

1 Front vise (Veritas Tools by Lee Valley Tools #70G08.02)

1 Twin-screw vise (Veritas Tools by Lee Valley Tools #05G12.22)

4 Bench dogs (Veritas Tools by Lee Valley Tools #05G04.04)

STEP 1 Rip and crosscut the eight horizontal supports A at 1½"-square by 24"-long, and the six vertical supports B at 1½"-square by 33½"-long. A good crosscut blade on a table saw will be required to cut the 1½"-thick material. A sliding table on your table saw, a radial-arm saw or power miter box can be used to crosscut the parts.

STEP 2 The eight horizontal supports A each require three dadoes that are 1"-wide by ½"-deep. Two of the dadoes are located 3" from each end, and the third is located directly in the center. Dadoes can be cut on a table saw. If possible, gang four pieces together at one time and mark the pairs; this will ensure that sets are matched for joining.

STEP 3 Glue two horizontal supports A together, forming a board with three 1"-square through-mortises. The eight supports will make four horizontal support members. Use dowels, biscuits or simply edge-glue the pieces to each other.

STEP 4 The six vertical supports B require a 1"-square by 1½"-long tenon centered on each end. These tenons can be cut on a table saw with a miter slide or, if you have one, a tenoning jig.

STEP 5 Cut a 45° corner on the end of all four horizontal supports A. Use a ¼" roundover bit in your router to ease all the corners on the vertical supports B, and the top edges of the bottom two horizontal supports A. Don't round over the bottom of the lower horizontal supports that touch the floor or the two top horizontal supports.

STEP 6 Build both leg assemblies using glue and clamps. The tenons should fit snugly into the mortises. Set aside both leg units until the adhesive cures.

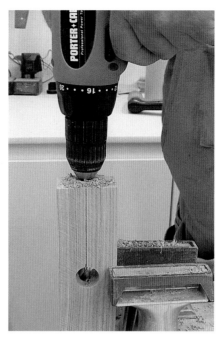

STEP 8 Cut the two stretcher boards D to the size indicated in the materials list. Drill a 1"-diameter through-hole, centered 4" from each end on both stretchers. Then drill the ends of both boards using a ⅜"-diameter bit. The holes are located on the center of each end and are drilled 4" deep to meet the 1"-diameter through-holes.

STEP 7 To save wear and tear on the lower horizontal supports, install sacrifice pads. These are 3"-square by 1"-thick and are attached with screws only. When the pads wear because the bench is moved a great deal or become damaged by moisture or liquids on the floor, simply replace the pads.

STEP 9 Drill a ½"-deep by 1"-diameter hole 4" above the bottom of each vertical support B. Center the hole on the four vertical uprights, making sure your measurements are from the bottom of the vertical supports and not the lower edge of the horizontal supports. Next, drill a ⅜"-diameter through-hole in the center of each 1"-diameter hole for the assembly bolts. Attach both leg assemblies together using the two stretchers. Use 4"-long by ⅜"-diameter bolts and washers to secure the base. The 1" hole on the outside of each vertical support will allow you to recess the bolt head, and the 1"-diameter through-hole in the stretcher board D will be used to attach the nuts to the bolts.

STEP 10 Cut the drawer carcass parts as detailed in the materials list. I am using ¾"-thick oak veneer plywood to contrast the solid ash.

Apply wood edge tape to all front and top edges of the side boards E. The backboard H requires edge tape on the top and both side edges, as do the front edges of boards F.

Use a router to cut a ¼"-deep by 1½"-wide dado in the center inside face of both top and bottom boards for the dividers.

STEP 11 I used three #20 biscuits and glue to attach the carcass sides E to the bottom and top boards F. Dowels or screws and glue can also be used.

STEP 12 Apply glue to both dadoes and place the dividers G into those dadoes. Use a heavy weight on top of the carcass until the adhesive sets and the dividers are fixed solidly n place.

I'm using two dividers for strength because I don't want the dividers to flex, which may interfere with the drawer runners if a lot of weight is added to the top board of the carcass. It's possibly overbuilt at this point, but I'd rather have more support than needed instead of just enough.

STEP 13 The backboard H is attached with #20 biscuits and glue. Clamp it in place until the adhesive sets up.

STEP 14 Put the drawer carcass in the bench frame. Rest the bottom board on both stretchers, aligning the backboard with the outside face of the back stretcher. Use 1½" PB screws to secure the carcass to the bench frame. Do not use glue, so it can be removed if the bench must be moved.

STEP 15 I'm installing drawers on both sides of the carcass. One side will have three drawers and the other side two.

Calculating drawer sizes means subtracting 1" from the interior carcass width for most drawer glides. However, it's well worth purchasing your glides at this point to verify the installation instructions.

In a frameless-style cabinet, such as this one, drawer height is found by following a few simple rules. Each drawer box should have 1" clearance above and below. That required space means there will be a 2" space between drawer boxes. The interior space is 18½" high, meaning on a two-drawer bank we must subtract 4" from that height (1" above and below each drawer box for purposes of calculating drawer height), and divide the result by two. The drawer height for the two-drawer bank will be 18½" minus 4" divided by 2, or 7¼" high.

The same calculations apply to the three-drawer bank. The drawer boxes will be 18½" minus 6" divided by 3, or approximately 4⅛" high, to provide the correct clearance.

Cut all the drawer parts to size as detailed in the materials list. These boxes will be constructed using ½" baltic birch plywood.

STEP 16 Each drawer box side J and M will need a rabbet cut ½" wide by ¼" deep on each inside face at both ends. The back and front boards will fit into these rabbets. Use a router table or table saw to make the cuts.

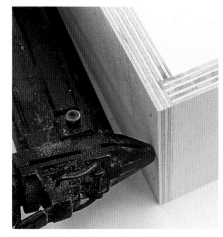

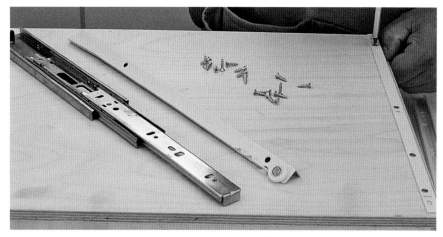

STEP 17 Join the drawer box sides to the back and front boards using glue and 1" brad nails. The nails will hold the joint until the glue dries. Glue and nail the bottom boards to the drawer box frames.

STEP 18 Attach drawer runners to each box. I am using ¾-extension glides, but full-extension glides (silver in the photo) can also be used if you require full access to the drawer. The full-extension models are two to three times more expensive than the ¾-extension type, but worth the extra cost if you need to fully access the drawer box.

Attach the runners using ½" screws and follow the manufacturer's instructions.

STEP 19 Mount the cabinet runners using a level line as a guide, or with a drawer glide-mounting jig.

Install one glide at the bottom of each cabinet section, and one 8" above the bottom board in the two-drawer cabinet. The three-drawer section has one set of runners at the bottom, one at 7" above the bottom board, and the top runner set 14" above the bottom.

STEP 20 The drawer faces Q, R and S are made using ¾"-thick veneer plywood. All four edges of each drawer face have wood veneer tape applied.

STEP 21 Here's an easy way to accurately locate drawer faces. First, drill the handle hole (or holes) in the drawer face, not through the drawer box at this point. Position the drawer face against the cabinet with the drawer box in place. Once located, drive a wood screw through the handle hole and into the drawer box until the face is secure. Next, open the drawer and drive 1" screws through the back of the drawer box front board, into the drawer face. Finally, remove the screws from the handle holes, drill holes completely through the box and install the handles or knobs.

STEP 22 My benchtop T is constructed using six 5½"-wide boards that are 1½" thick. The boards are left longer than 72" and will be trimmed to size once the top is sanded. Thick boards can be joined with a double-biscuit technique that's shown in the photo.

STEP 23 To prepare rough boards for joining, flatten one face on a jointer.

STEP 24 Next, press the flat face against the jointer fence and mill one edge at 90° to the prepared face.

STEP 25 Cut the remaining rough edge parallel to the jointed edge, and at 90° to the prepared face, on a table saw. Hold the jointed edge of the board tight to the saw fence and the prepared face flat on the saw table.

STEP 26 Use a planer to dress the rough face parallel to the prepared face. The board is now ready to be joined to other boards.

STEP 27 Join the boards with clamps on the top and bottom face as shown. This over-and-under technique will help to ensure that your top will set up flat. Tighten the clamps until you see just a little of the glue squeeze out. Clamps set too tight will squeeze out a lot of glue, starving the joint and possibly making it fail.

STEP 28 Complete the top by scraping off the excess glue and sanding smooth. Trim to the required 30"-wide by 72"-long size. Turn the top facedown on the floor. Set the leg and carcass assembly upside down on the bottom face of the top so it's equally spaced side to side and front to back. Drill small pilot holes through the upper horizontal support and into the top. One hole at the end of each support is required.

STEP 29 Drill 1"-diameter holes, 1" deep, in the bottom face of the top using the small drill holes from the previous step as a guide. Cut and install four 2½"-long by 1"-diameter dowels in the holes using glue.

Drill 1"-diameter holes completely through the upper horizontal supports using the pilot holes as a guide. Once the adhesive sets, put the top on the base assembly with the dowels set into the four holes. You may need to widen the diameter of the horizontal support holes with sandpaper to install the top.

STEP 30 My front vise is a single-screw model made by Veritas Tools, available from Lee Valley Tools. I followed the installation instructions and added two 1½"-thick wood jaws.

STEP 31 The end vise I used is also made by Veritas and is a twin-screw model. When using large end vises on this bench, be sure the moving mechanics of the vise clear the bench supports. I used 7¼"-high wood jaws, centering the screws 3" up from the bottom edge of the boards, so both screws would clear the upper horizontal supports.

CONSTRUCTION
notes

I drilled ¾"-diameter holes in my bench-top to accommodate round bench dogs. Both vise jaws also had ¾"-diameter holes drilled for the round dogs. These bench dogs can be used with either vise to clamp flat boards that need to be sanded or planed.

The size of this bench, the number of drawers in the storage carcass, the height and the accessory equipment can all be modified to suit your requirements. My bench is 36" high, but that may not be suitable for everyone. If this plan isn't right for you, change the dimensions.

Hardwood is an excellent choice for any workbench. A bench will be around for many years, and may be passed to future generations of woodworkers, so use the best quality hardwood you can afford.

I finished my bench with three coats of oil-based polyurethane that is commonly used on hardwood floors. I gave the top a good coat of hard paste wax to further protect the surface from liquids and adhesive spills.

This is a great project. I hope you'll enjoy your new workbench as much as I enjoy mine.

Fold-away Work Center

This project is all about secure storage and a solid worktable that sets up quickly — but it's also about cost. This work center, with a solid table and lockable storage for tools and supplies, can be built for $75 or less.

I used two sheets of ¾"-thick medium-density fiberboard (MDF) to build the cabinet and bench. However, if you're not fond of MDF, you can use any sheet material. The real plus with MDF is its low cost; the downside is its weight. The worktable weighs nearly 100 pounds, so that might be a consideration. The two-layer MDF worktable sandwich is flat, stable and sturdy, but you'll have to use a little extra caution when lifting it into a horizontal position. Plywood is quite a bit lighter, but it's also a lot more expensive. I like MDF for workshop cabinets because of the low cost, smooth work surface and weight, which tends to stabilize tables and cabinetry.

The table drops almost flat against a wall, and the folding cabinet is only 8" deep when closed. Tool and material storage is right above the workbench for quick access. When you're ready to work on a project, open the wings of the locked cabinet, raise the bench and lock the supports, install the cross brace and you're set to go. You will be able to set up and break down the center in less than two minutes. No time is wasted dragging tables around the garage or looking for tools.

My favorite feature is the security provided by this project. Valuable and sometimes dangerous tools or equipment can be locked in a cabinet that only you can

open. A garage workshop isn't the most secure place, because children can get at sharp chisels or supplies they shouldn't be handling. Well-meaning neighbors sometimes borrow tools that are lying around the garage, and items often have a habit of disappearing. This fold-away work center eliminates these problems

and ensures that your tools and supplies are always where you left them.

I'm sure you'll find this project useful in a shop where you share space. It's easy and inexpensive to build. Once it's installed, move the car outside and you'll be ready to work wood in a couple of minutes!

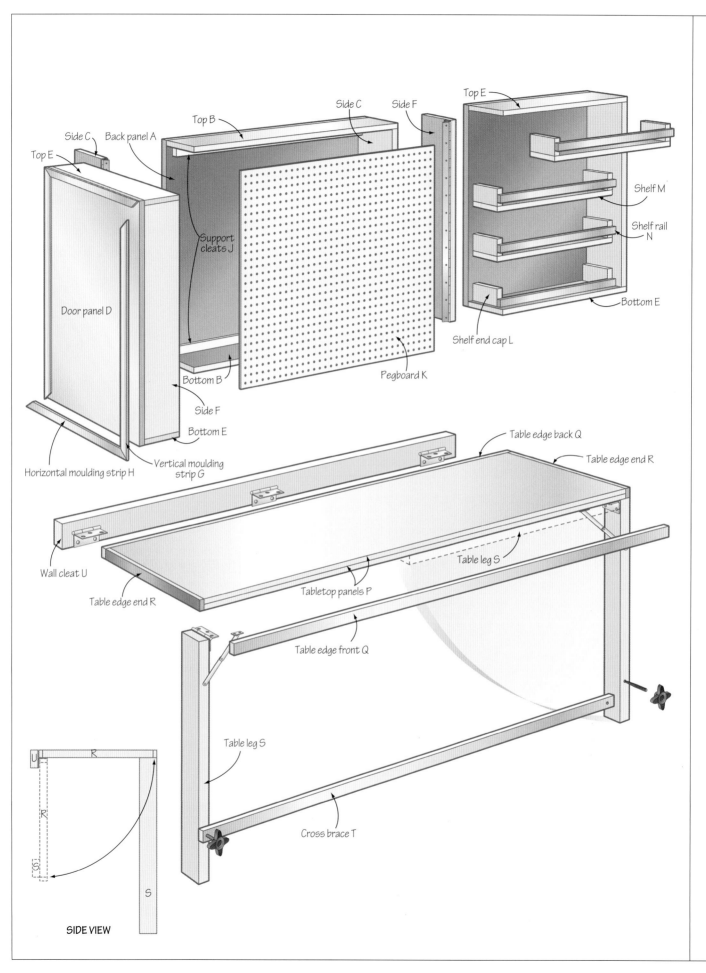

Side C

Top E

Top B

Side C

Side F

Top E

Side C

Back panel A

Support cleats J

Door panel D

Shelf M

Shelf rail N

Bottom E

Shelf end cap L

Pegboard K

Bottom B

Side F

Bottom E

Vertical moulding strip G

Horizontal moulding strip H

Table edge back Q

Table edge end R

Table leg S

Wall cleat U

Tabletop panels P

Table edge end R

Table edge front Q

Table leg S

Cross brace T

SIDE VIEW

U

R

R

S

S

Schedule of Materials: Fold-away Work Center

LTR.	NO.	ITEM	STOCK	INCHES T	(MM) T	INCHES W	(MM) W	INCHES L	(MM) L
A	1	back panel	MDF	¾	(19)	30	(762)	36	(914)
B	2	top and bottom	MDF	¾	(19)	4	(102)	36	(914)
C	2	sides	MDF	¾	(19)	4	(102)	28½	(724)
D	2	door panels	MDF	¾	(19)	30	(762)	17¹⁵⁄₁₆	(456)
E	4	top and bottom	MDF	¾	(19)	4	(102)	17¹⁵⁄₁₆	(456)
F	4	sides	MDF	¾	(19)	4	(102)	28½	(724)
G	4	vertical moulding strips	pine	¼	(6)	1¼	(32)	30	(762)
H	4	horizontal moulding strips	pine	¼	(6)	1¼	(32)	18	(457)
J	2	support cleats	plywood	½	(13)	1	(25)	34½	(876)
K	1	pegboard panel	hardboard	¼	(6)	28½	(724)	34½	(876)
L	16	shelf end caps	MDF	¾	(19)	3½	(89)	3½	(89)
M	6	shelf boards	MDF	¾	(19)	3½	(89)	16½	(419)
N	8	shelf rails	pine	¼	(6)	1¼	(32)	16½	(419)
P	2	tabletop panels	MDF	¾	(19)	24	(610)	70½	(1791)
Q	2	table edges front and back	hardwood	¾	(19)	1½	(38)	72	(1829)
R	2	table end edges	hardwood	¾	(19)	1½	(38)	24	(610)
S	2	table legs	pine	1½	(38)	3½	(89)	34½	(876)
T	1	cross brace	hardwood	¾	(19)	1½	(38)	72	(1829)
U	1	wall cleat	pine	1½	(38)	3½	(89)	72	(1829)

Supplies

5 Sets of 18"-long, ¾-extension glides (use full-extension glides if desired)

Drawer handles or knobs

PB screws

Bolts, nuts and washers as detailed

Plate joinery biscuits (#20)

Glue

4" x ⅜"-Diameter bolts with washers and nuts

Wood edge tape

1½" PB screws

1" Brad nails

½" Screws

1" Screws

Optional

1   Front vise (Veritas Tools by Lee Valley Tools #70G08.02)

1   Twin-screw vise (Veritas Tools by Lee Valley Tools #05G12.22)

4   Bench dogs (Veritas Tools by Lee Valley Tools #05G04.04)

SHOP tip

MDF can easily split when driving screws. Here are a couple of tips to minimize damage to the board. First, always predrill screw holes before driving screws into the boards. To further eliminate splits, extend the drill bit so the pilot hole will be at least $^1/_8$" longer than the screw shaft. Finally, stay at least 1" away from board ends when installing screws.

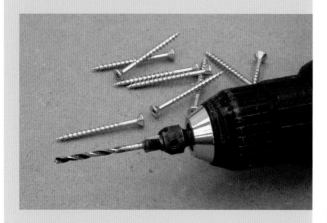

STEP 1 Cut the back panel A as well as the top and bottom B and sides C to the sizes indicated in the materials list. The four panels B and C are attached to the back panel A with glue and 1½"-long screws as shown in the illustration. These four panels are aligned with the outside edges of the back panel. Drive screws through the rear face of the back panel into the B and C panel edges, spacing them about 6" apart, but first be sure to drill pilot holes in the MDF. Glue and a screw should also be used at each corner where the side, top and bottom boards meet. If you have a plate joiner and prefer biscuits instead of screws, use No. 20s to join the panels, but you'll have to clamp all the joints until the adhesive sets. Remember, screws will not be seen on the rear face of panel A after the cabinet is installed.

STEP 2 Build two doors following the same assembly procedure as in step 1, using panels D, E and F. Each door width is $^1/_{16}$" narrower than one-half the total cabinet width. That dimension will provide a $^1/_8$" gap between the doors when mounted. Use glue and 1½" screws in pilot holes to build the wing doors.

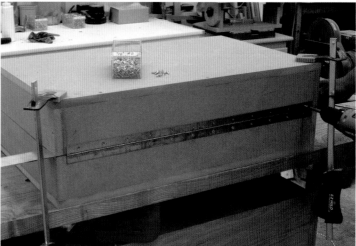

STEP 3 Attach each door case to the backboard case using a 28"-or 30"-long piano hinge. I've installed the hinges on the outside face of each box instead of the normal inside edge. An MDF edge will not offer as much hold for the screws as the panel face, so I decided this was a better method for hinge installation. While you install the hinges, temporarily place a $^1/_{16}$" spacer between the backboard and wing doors so the doors will operate without binding. Use a $^5/_8$"- or ¾"-long coarse-threaded screw to secure the hinges, filling each hinge hole with a screw.

STEP 5 You can configure the inside of the wall case in a number of ways. The interior shelves and tool holders should be designed to meet your requirements. I'll detail one possible design that you may find useful. First, install two support cleats J, which will support the ¼" pegboard in the center section. These cleats are installed at the top and bottom of the case to provide space for the hangers to poke out behind the pegboard. Use any ½"-thick stock that you have lying around the shop, as the cleats will not be visible. Glue and a few brad nails will secure the cleats.

STEP 4 Install moulding strips G and H on both front panels D of the swing doors. I used a standard lumber supply moulding called Parclose, which is readily available. Use glue and brad nails to attach the moulding, joining the corners with 45° miters. The moulding is not a necessary structural item; however, the moulding hides screw heads and adds a little visual interest to the case.

STEP 6 Attach a pegboard panel K to the cleats with 1¼"-long screws and decorative washers. Three screws in the top and bottom cleat will secure the panel.

STEP 8 Install a barrel bolt on the inside of one door. It will secure the door and prevent movement when a latch and lock is installed. Attach a small square of wood with glue and 1½" screws on the door's inside edge to mount the bolt assembly. Close the door, mark where the slide bolt touches the cabinet's bottom board and drill a hole for the barrel.

STEP 7 I'm installing shelves in each door. They are made using ¾"-thick MDF and strips of Parclose moulding. The shelves are built using the end caps L and shelf boards M. The rails N keep the materials and supplies from falling off the shelves. Each assembly is attached to the door sides with one screw. I didn't use glue so that I can move the shelves in case my storage requirements change. The moulding rails are attached with glue and brad nails. The bottom rack or shelf assembly doesn't require a shelf board.

STEP 9 Attach a lock hasp assembly to the doors. You may have to chisel and form the perimeter moulding to mount the hasp. Buy the hardware, hold it in place and mark its position. A little trimming of the moulding should be all that's needed to mount the latch.

SHOP tip

You will get both workbench top panels from one sheet of MDF. It typically comes in sheets that measure 49" by 97", so there should be plenty of material for the saw kerf (width of the blade cut in material). Be careful handling ¾" MDF because a full sheet weighs almost 100 pounds and the workbench top sandwich is a full sheet. Get some help to move it around if necessary.

STEP 10 Cut the two tabletop panels P to create a 1½"-thick workbench top. Put standard white or yellow glue on the face of one panel and then lay the other on top, being sure to align the edges. Clamp the panel sandwich and drive 1¼" screws into the bottom face to hold the panels together until the glue sets properly.

STEP 11 Attach the four hardwood edge strips Q and R to the MDF panels. I attached my hardwood edges with glue and 1½" screws in ⅜"-diameter counterbored holes. After the screws were installed, I filled the holes with wood plugs. You can also attach the edge strips with biscuits, dowels, splines or by simply gluing and clamping. Use whichever method makes you most comfortable.

STEP 12 The top surface of my workbench top will be 36" high because I find that height comfortable. The leg heights can be changed to suit your height preference. Cut the two legs S to the size shown in the materials list. Use 3" butt hinges to attach the legs to the underside of the workbench top, as shown, at each end. Test the folded position of the legs, making sure they lie flat and do not contact each other.

SHOP tip

When all the leg and wall cleat hardware is attached, the table underside should look as shown in the photograph. Once the table is mounted on the wall, the underside will not be visible, or easily accessible, so be sure the legs and wall cleat operate properly.

STEP 13 Purchase and install folding supports for each leg. In many cases, there are right- and left-side supports, so check the package labels when you buy the hardware. Install the supports following the manufacturer's instructions.

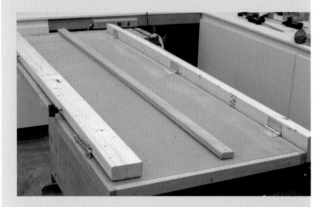

STEP 14 To increase the stability of the legs, install the cross brace T. The brace is attached to each leg with hanger bolts and threaded knobs for quick installation and removal. Use 2½"-long threaded hanger bolts and the proper knobs. Drill holes at each end of the cross brace for the hanger bolts. Locate the rail near the middle of each leg.

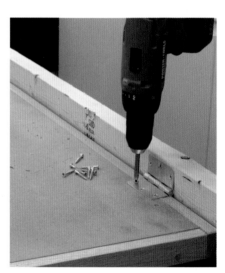

STEP 15 The workbench will be supported on the wall by a cleat. This wall cleat U is a 6' length of construction-grade framing lumber. The table is attached to the wall cleat using 3" butt hinges and 1¼"-long screws. The wall cleat's top edge, when attached to the wall, is aligned flush with the top surface of the workbench top.

SHOP tip

If your garage or basement floor is uneven, as mine is, install adjustable feet on the table legs. The feet are available at hardware stores. Or you could vary each leg length to match your floor based on a level tabletop. Another simple method would be to cut a block to the correct thickness to shim the leg.

CONSTRUCTION notes

As I often mention in these construction notes, material choice is a secondary issue. If you'd prefer to work with plywood instead of MDF, don't hesitate. Material choice is a matter of personal preference, so use what you are most comfortable working with and what is right for the conditions. For example, some garage workshops are damp and subject to water leaks, so I'd consider a water-resistant sheet material or at least one that I could paint to offer added protection.

The wall cabinet size should also be modified to suit your needs. You may want to store expensive power tools or small hand tools, so build the cabinet to meet those requirements. Each door wing is normally one-half the back cabinet width, less ¹⁄₁₆". It's easy to calculate the panel measurements for a 40"-wide cabinet with two 19¹⁵⁄₁₆" doors, and so on.

The wall cabinet height above the workbench is usually in the 12" to 18" range, but that's not a fixed rule. Your woodworking interests may require more space between the bench top and cabinet, so raise it to the height you need.

Finally, there's the issue of bench height. I know of no rule that demands a specific height. The leg length can be any height to meet the needs of someone short or tall. You might want to use a stool at the bench if you do a lot of woodcarving or scroll sawing. If that's the case, remember the rule of 12s, which states the stool seat height should be 12" less than the bench top surface height. A 36"-high bench top would require a 24"-high stool, and so on.

STEP 16 Secure the wall cabinet to any wall by driving 3" screws through the pegboard and into the wall studs 12" to 18" above the bench top surface. Be sure the cabinet is level and plumb. The wall cleat U is attached to wall studs with 3" wood screws. The top edge of the cleat will be level and set at 36" above the floor.

Adjustable Worktable

Woodworkers often work on many types of projects throughout the year. One week it will be a small craft or carving project, and the next one might be a bathroom cabinet. A high worktable is great when working on small projects, but that same table is almost useless when building a cabinet case.

You could build two benches, one high and the other low, but most of us don't have that kind of room available. Why not build a worktable that can be raised and lowered to suit each requirement? Well, if you do a wide range of large and small projects, this worktable may be your solution to achieving a proper, and comfortable, workbench height.

This adjustable worktable can be fixed at 24" or 40" high and everything in between at 1½" increments. It's strong, with a heavy top that's perfectly flat, and has a replaceable surface. You can, as I did, add a pullout tool tray for small hand tools.

The adjustable-height feature is a bonus in many custom cabinet shops. A fixed-height bench means you're either bending over to work on small carvings or reaching over your head to assemble large cabinets. Both situations can be very tiring and a strain on your back. Fixing the table height at a comfortable level for the project you're currently building will add a great deal of enjoyment and comfort for any woodworker.

The "sandwiched" top, using ¾" particleboard, is heavy, so if you don't have someone to help change the table's height, I'll show you how to safely adjust it by yourself. The particleboard top, low-cost pine 2×4s, a few screws, hardware and glue make this an affordable project in the $150 to $200 range, depending on the cost of materials in your area.

Before starting, look at the scissor jack lift option at the end of this chapter. If you plan to change the height frequently, this system might be right for you. The scissor jack should be purchased first, as its dimensions might determine rail positions for your bench.

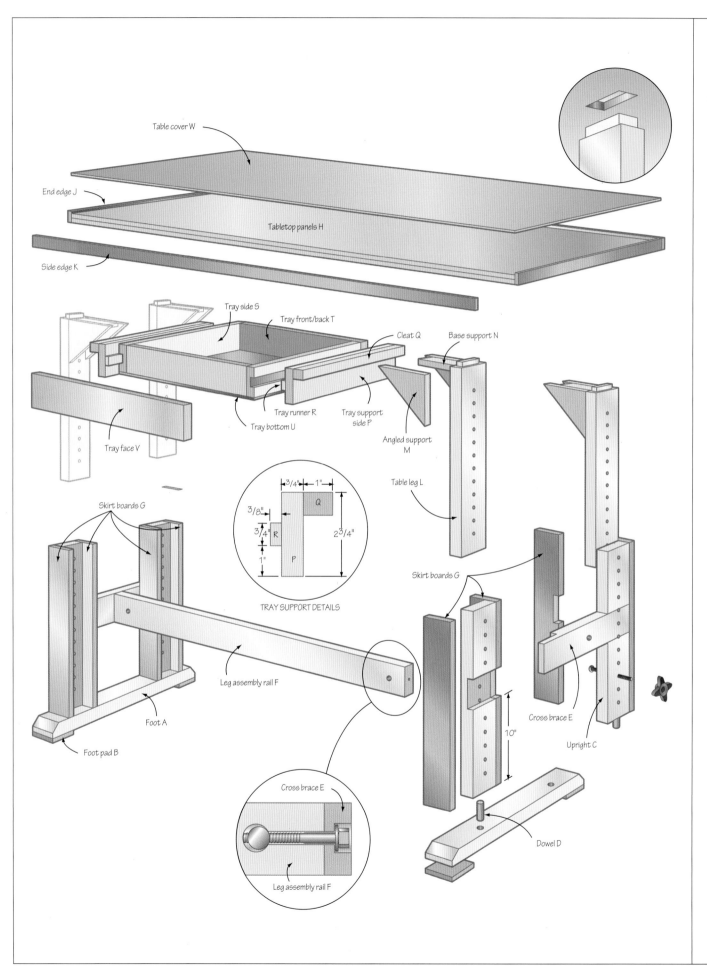

Table cover W

End edge J

Tabletop panels H

Side edge K

Tray side S

Tray front/back T

Cleat Q

Base support N

Tray runner R

Tray support side P

Tray bottom U

Angled support M

Tray face V

Table leg L

Skirt boards G

3/4" 1"

3/8"

3/4" R

Q

2 3/4"

1" P

TRAY SUPPORT DETAILS

Skirt boards G

Leg assembly rail F

Cross brace E

Foot A

Upright C

Foot pad B

10"

Cross brace E

Dowel D

Leg assembly rail F

Schedule of Materials: Adjustable Worktable

LTR.	NO.	ITEM	STOCK	INCHES T	(MM) T	INCHES W	(MM) W	INCHES L	(MM) L
A	2	feet	solid wood	1⅝	(41)	3½	(89)	28	(711)
B	4	foot pads	plywood	1/2	(13)	3½	(89)	3½	(89)
C	4	uprights	solid wood	1⅝	(41)	3½	(89)	20	(508)
D	4	dowels	solid wood	1" dia.	(25)			3	(76)
E	2	cross braces	solid wood	1⅝	(41)	3½	(89)	21	(533)
F	1	leg assembly rail	solid wood	1⅝	(41)	3½	(89)	55	(1397)
G	8	skirt boards	solid wood	¾	(19)	3½	(89)	20	(508)
H	2	tabletop panels	particleboard	¾	(19)	27	(686)	72	(1829)
J	2	end edges	solid wood	¾	(19)	1¾	(45)	27	(686)
K	2	side edges	solid wood	¾	(19)	1¾	(45)	73½	(1867)
L	4	table legs	solid wood	1⅝	(41)	31/2	(89)	20¾	(527)
M	8	angled supports	particleboard	¾	(19)	61/2	(165)	6½	(165)
N	4	base supports	particleboard	¾	(19)	2	(51)	5½	(140)
P	2	tray support sides	particleboard	¾	(19)	2¾	(70)	18	(457)
Q	2	cleats	hardwood	¾	(19)	1	(25)	18	(457)
R	2	tray runners	hardwood	⅜	(10)	¾	(19)	18	(457)
S	2	tray sides	particleboard	¾	(19)	2¼	(57)	18	(457)
T	2	tray front & back	particleboard	¾	(19)	2¼	(57)	22½	(572)
U	1	tray bottom	plywood	¼	(6)	18	(457)	22	(559)
V	1	tray face	solid wood	¾	(19)	3½	(89)	28	(711)
W	1	table cover	hardboard	¼	(6)	27	(686)	72	(1829)

Supplies

1¼" (32mm) Screws

1½" (38mm) Screws

2" (51mm) Screws

3" (76mm) Screws

Brad nails

Small nails or double-sided tape

Glue

2 ⅜" x 5" (10mm x 127mm) Bolts, nuts and washers

8 ¼" x 4" (6mm x 102mm) Carriage bolts

8 Fender washers

8 ¼" (6mm) Diameter threaded knobs

SHOP tip

You can cut dadoes using a standard blade on your table saw or with a circular saw. First, make a series of kerf cuts, about ¼" apart, along the dado width. Next, use a hammer and sharp chisel to clean the waste from the cut.

STEP 1 Cut the two feet A to the size shown in the materials list. Both ends of each foot can be mitered with a 45° cut on the top face, 1" back from the ends. This technique adds visual interest to the legs and removes any sharp corners.

STEP 2 The two feet should have foot pads B installed at both ends. They can be changed as they wear or are damaged but, more importantly, will help to stabilize the table on rough floors. Attach each pad with two 1½" long screws, but don't use glue here.

STEP 3 The four uprights C require a dado starting 10" above the bottom end. These dadoes are ¹³⁄₁₆" deep (or half the thickness of the material used) and 3½" wide. Cut the dadoes with a stacked dado head cutter on your table saw. Or, see the shop tip that explains how to cut these dadoes using a standard blade on your table saw or circular saw.

STEP 4 The uprights C are positioned 3½" from each foot end. Draw a line from corner to corner on the bottom end of each upright to determine the center point. Trace the upright outline and position on the feet, holding the back face of each upright flush with the back or outside edge of each foot. Draw lines on the traced rectangles to determine their center points.

STEP 5 At this point you can drill a 1"-diameter hole at the marked center point of each foot and upright. However, it's difficult to drill straight holes by hand in separate pieces to be joined. I suggest that you attach the uprights to the feet using glue and two 3"-long screws through the bottom face of the feet and into the uprights. These screws will hold the upright-to-foot connection while we proceed with the next step.

STEP 6 Drill a 1"-diameter hole, 3" deep, through the foot and into the upright end. Try to hold the drill as straight as possible. Drive a 1"- diameter by 3"-long wood dowel D into the hole. Apply glue to the dowels before driving them into the holes.

STEP 7 Cut the two cross braces E to size. Form a $^{13}/_{16}$"-deep by 3½"- wide rabbet on each end. The cross braces fit between the uprights and are secured in the dadoes with glue and two 1¼" long screws.

STEP 8 The leg assembly rail F joins the two leg assemblies by attaching to the cross braces. Drill a 1½"-diameter hole 3½" from each leg rail end. Be sure to center the holes on the 3½"-wide face of the rail. Clamp the rail between the two leg assemblies flush with the top edges of the cross braces and centered 10½" from each end. Carefully drill ⅜"-diameter holes through the cross braces into the leg rail center. The holes should exit on one edge of the 1½"-diameter holes in the leg rail. Use ⅜"-diameter by 5"-long bolts with nuts and washers to secure the leg rail to each of the leg assemblies.

STEP 9 Once the bolts are tight and the leg rail is secured to the cross braces, drive two 3" long wood screws into each end above and below the bolts. These will not add a great deal of holding power as they are driven into leg rail end grain, but will act as pins to stop the rail from twisting. Don't use glue on these connections, so the table can be dismantled for moving.

STEP 10 Each upright will have two skirt boards. These skirts will form a channel for the tabletop legs and help to stabilize the table in its various adjusted positions. Cut the eight skirt boards G and attach them to the uprights with glue and 1½"-long screws. Install the outside skirt boards first because the inner skirts require a notch to fit around the cross braces.

STEP 11 The remaining four inside skirt boards require a notch, as discussed in the previous step. The notch is 1⅝"deep by 3½" wide and aligned, beginning 10" from the bottom edge, to the cross braces. Notch the boards on a table saw with a dado blade or use the procedure described in the next shop tip.

SHOP tip

As you can see in the photograph for step 11, I have gang clamped the boards together for the notch cut. This technique should be used when cutting a number of boards to ensure they are all the same. It also reduces the amount of passes that have to be made on the saw.

If you don't have a table saw, use a jigsaw to cut the notches. A band saw can also be used, or they can be cut by hand.

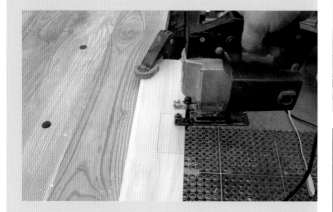

STEP 12 Install the inside skirt boards, using glue and three 1½" long screws.

STEP 14 The edges of the sheet material are banded with ¾"-thick wood. I will be adding a ¼"-thick hardboard (called tempered or Masonite board) as a replaceable top, so the wood used to edge the top will be 1¾" high. The wood edges J and K can be attached with biscuits, screws in counterbored holes filled with plugs, or screws with the heads flush to the edge surface. Pick a method that suits you, but use glue as part of the fastening system. Cut the edges J and K. Attach the strips ¼" above the table top surface using a guide that's the same thickness as the top material.

STEP 13 Put the base aside for now and cut the two ¾"-thick tabletop panels H, which measure 27" wide by 72" long. I'm using ¾"-thick particleboard, but any sheet material can be used to build the top. Glue the two sheets together. Be sure they are accurately aligned to each other and clamp tightly until the adhesive sets up. You might also want to add some weight in the middle to ensure a good bond.

STEP 15 Turn the tabletop upside down and center the base on the top. Trace the inside perimeter of the uprights and skirt boards on the underside of the top. These lines will indicate where the table legs will be positioned.

STEP 16 Next, use a scrap piece of 1⅝" x 3½" stock to trace the final line for the leg positions.

STEP 17 Cut the four table legs L to the size indicated on the materials list. They are the same size as the base uprights with an added ¾", which will be used for a tenon on one end. Use a stacked dado cutter on your table saw, or a standard blade, to cut a ¼" deep by ¾"-wide rabbet on all four faces of each leg. Those cuts will form a tenon that's 1⅛" wide by 3" long on one end of the four legs.

STEP 18 Use the leg outlines that were previously drawn to mark the mortise position. Draw lines ¼" inside the rectangles to define the cut lines for the four mortises. Use a flat-bottomed drill bit (1" in diameter) to remove most of the waste. Each mortise is ¾" deep, so mark the drill depth position on your bit. Use a sharp chisel to remove the remaining waste. The finished mortises should be ¾"deep by 1⅛" wide by 3" long.

STEP 19 Before applying glue to the leg tenons, build the four support brackets. They are made with two pieces of angled supports M cut at 45°, and a base support N that spans the two angled supports. Cut parts M and N, then use glue with 2"-long screws to assemble the leg braces.

STEP 20 Use glue and 3"-long screws to attach the brackets to the legs. The base supports N will rest on the tabletop, so align the bracket with the top end of the tenon.

STEP 21 Apply glue to the leg tenons and bracket bottoms. Use 2"-long screws through the base support N to secure the legs to the table.

STEP 22 Place the base assembly on the table, sliding the skirts over the legs. Drill ¼"-diameter holes through the uprights and legs. Make a template with holes spaced 1¼" on center beginning 1" from the bottom of the uprights and end 1" above the tabletop.

STEP 23 The lower section is attached to the upper section with ¼"-diameter by 4"-long carriage bolts, a large fender washer, and a threaded knob. All the hardware is available at most home centers. Each leg/upright has two bolt assemblies that are located in different holes as the table height is adjusted.

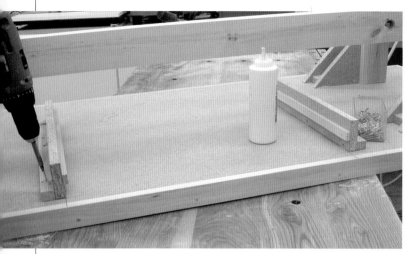

STEP 24 The tool tray case and support assembly can be built with sheet material left over after cutting the tabletop panels. My tool tray is 18" deep by 24" wide and 3½" high. The tray support sides P are 2¾"high with a 1"-wide cleat Q on the outside face and a ⅜"-thick by ¾"-high tray runner R on the inside face. The tray runners begin 1" above the bottom edge of sides P and are secured with glue and brad nails. Set the two support sides 1½" behind the table edge. Secure both assemblies with glue and 2" screws so the tray will be centered on the table. The inside dimension, or inside support side face to inside support side face, must be 24¹/₁₆" to accommodate the tool tray case.

STEP 25 Assemble the tool tray using parts S, T and U. The corners are joined with simple butt joints, glue and 2"-long screws. The tray box sides S require a ¹³/₁₆"-wide groove that's ⅜" deep to slide on the runners R. Be sure to locate the screws as close to the top and bottom as possible so they won't be in the groove path. Attach the ¼" plywood bottom U using glue and brad nails.

STEP 26 Cut a ¹³/₁₆"-wide by ⅜"-deep groove along each side of the tool tray. The groove begins 1" above the tray's bottom. Use a stacked dado cutter on your table saw or a router bit to cut the groove.

STEP 27 The tray face V is a piece of ¾" solid wood. It's wide enough to cover the support assembles and act as a stop. Align the face with the tool tray centered from side to side and ¼" higher than the tray's top edge. Use three 1¼" long screws, through the back face of the front tray board, to secure the face. The amount of material hanging below the tray can be used as a handle.

STEP 28 The table cover W is ¼"-thick hardboard. It can be attached to the table with small nails or double-sided tape. When necessary, the cover can be reversed or replaced, so don't use any adhesive when installing the cover.

Adjusting the Table Height Manually

STEP 1 Adjusting the table height with two people is relatively easy. However, if you work alone as I do most of the time, you'll need an easy way to change the height. I first remove the tool tray, then lay two 2x4s on the floor. The table can be tipped to rest on the 2x4s.

STEP 2 Tip the table on its top and adjust the legs to any height you require. Once the bolts are in place, turn the table right-side up.

Adjusting the Table Height Mechanically

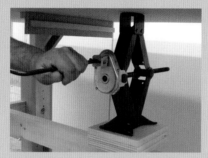

STEP 1 A scissor jack that can travel 16" vertically is used to adjust the table in an upright position. Purchase a jack that has a travel of 16", not one that has a maximum height of 16". Maximum-height dimensions given for scissor jacks include the height of the jack at rest. The fully closed scissor uses 4" to 5" of space and reduces the travel distance. The best way to check jack travel is to measure the top plate at rest, then crank it all the way up and measure the top plate's position. The difference should be at least 16". The jack should be located at the center of the table, measuring from side to side and front to back, for balanced lifting. Attach a plywood platform, a little larger than the scissor jack's footprint to the leg rail assembly. Use as many pieces of wood as required so the jack sits on the platform with its top plate touching the underside of the table when both (jack and worktable) are in the lowest position. The platform can be anchored with screws, and the scissor jack's base can be screwed to the platform. You may have to drill holes in the jack's metal foot for the screws.

STEP 2 Remove the bolts and knobs in the legs and turn the jack handle until the desired height is reached. Replace the bolts in their new holes and lock the table. Scissor jacks with a minimum of 16" travel are often available at auto supply stores, but they can be found at all recreational vehicle (RV) accessory stores. These jacks are commonly used to level RV trailers when parked. Installing the jack will affect drawer design and depth, so take that issue into consideration before building the drawer. This option may not be necessary for everyone, and the cost ($75 to $100) for a good scissor jack might make you reconsider this option, but if you need frequent height changes, it's well worth the money spent.

CONSTRUCTION
notes

I used furniture-grade pine for my uprights and legs. The tabletop was made with two layers of ¾"-thick particleboard. However, any 2x4 stock and sheet material can be substituted; it's your choice.

Particleboard sheet material is heavy and stable. The weight is a bonus because it keeps the table well anchored but does create problems when the table height has to be adjusted. However, I prefer a heavier table, and if I use the height changing method as shown, it's not too much of an inconvenience.

My tool tray is shallow because I plan to store chisels and rulers for easy access. You can easily change the depth and width to suit your needs as long as the depth isn't greater than the leg-rail-to-tabletop space when the table is fully lowered. You can also make two trays or drawers, using the same construction steps, by adding two tray runner supports.

The table height adjustment range is from 24" to 40". That should be suitable for most woodworking tasks but can be changed if you have special requirements. Remember, the height of the uprights, tabletop thickness, and foot assembly height determine the lowest tabletop height, so take those dimensions into consideration when designing your worktable.

Finally, you may need a wider or longer table. If so, change the tabletop panel dimensions as well as the leg rail length. Remember the rule of 12s for your bench. Should you want to sit at the worktable, use a chair or stool height that's 12" lower than the tabletop surface for comfortable seating.

Simple Sawhorses

I have tools in my shop that are worth hundreds of dollars. However, I can honestly say that these $5 sawhorses have been worth more to me than any tool on many occasions. They support cabinets during construction, quickly become a temporary workbench and make a great painting platform for my mouldings. More importantly, they save my back from wear and tear because they support my work at a comfortable level.

As you can see, these sawhorses are made with construction-grade lumber. If you want something a bit fancier, use a better grade of wood, but the cost rises dramatically. The only hardware involved is two carriage bolts, washers and wing nuts. This hardware can be used again when the time comes to build new sawhorses. Once the hardware is paid for, all you have to buy is a couple of 8' 2×4s.

One of the major advantages of this sawhorse design is the storage size. The feet can be quickly removed and attached flat to the legs. You can hang them on hooks in your garage or put them in the trunk of your car for transport to a job site. I usually have three or four sawhorses in my truck when I'm working at a client's house, because I know they'll be needed.

My sawhorses are beaten and bruised, covered in paint and stain, left in the rain and generally abused over the course of a year. So every once in a while I spend a couple of hours and build six or eight new units. I wouldn't be without these great helpers, and you won't either, once you build and use them in your workshop.

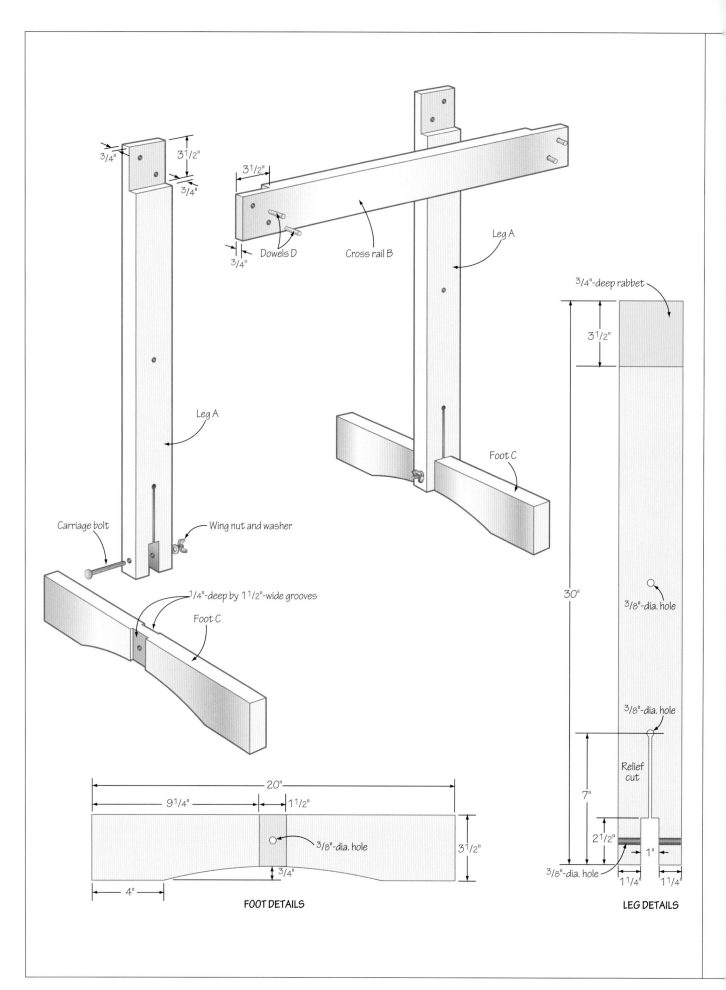

3/4"

3 1/2"

3/4"

3 1/2"

3/4"

Dowels D

Cross rail B

Leg A

3/4"-deep rabbet

3 1/2"

Leg A

Foot C

30"

3/8"-dia. hole

Carriage bolt

Wing nut and washer

3/8"-dia. hole

1/4"-deep by 1 1/2"-wide grooves

Foot C

Relief cut

7"

20"

2 1/2"

9 1/4"

1 1/2"

3/8"-dia. hole

1"

3 1/2"

3/4"

3/8"-dia. hole

4"

1 1/4"

1 1/4"

FOOT DETAILS

LEG DETAILS

Schedule of Materials: Simple Sawhorses

LTR.	NO.	ITEM	STOCK	INCHES T	(MM) T	INCHES W	(MM) W	INCHES L	(MM) L
A	2	legs	pine	1½	(38)	3½	(89)	30	(762)
B	1	cross rail	pine	1½	(38)	3½	(89)	30	(762)
C	2	feet	pine	1½	(38)	3½	(89)	30	(762)
D	4	dowels	hardwood	5⁄16 dia.	(8)			2	(51)

Supplies

2 5⁄16" x 4" (8mm x 102mm) Carriage bolts

2 5⁄16" (8mm) Washers

2 5⁄16" (8mm) Wing nuts

Glue

STEP 1 Cut the two legs A and the cross rail B to the sizes shown in the materials list. Set the rail on top of the legs, flush with the top edge, and draw reference lines to indicate the rabbet cut sizes and placement. You'll need one line on each leg and two on the cross rail.

STEP 2 The legs need a ¾"-deep by 3½"-long rabbet cut on the top end. The rail requires the same cut on each end. When joined, two rabbet cuts will form a half-lap joint. Set the outside face of your saw blade 3½" away from your saw fence. Use the miter slide in continuous passes to nibble away at the wood. If you have a dado blade for your saw, the process will be much quicker. You can also make the cuts with a band saw if you have one.

STEP 3 Apply glue to the rabbets, then clamp the leg and rail at the half-lap joints. Place scrap lumber under the joints as you will be installing dowels in drilled holes through each joint.

STEP 4 Drill two $5/16$"-diameter holes through each joint. Use 2"-long by $5/16$"-diameter dowels with glue applied and drive them through the joints. These dowels will be sanded flush once the glue dries.

STEP 5 Cut the feet C to size and form a 1½"-wide by ¼"-deep dado on
opposite faces, which will form a 1"-thick bridge on each foot. The dadoes
are located in the center of the feet. The dadoes can be cut on a table saw
with a standard or dado blade.

STEP 6 The feet require an arc, which starts 4" from each end and is ¾" high
in the center, to lessen contact points with the floor for better stability. Use a
template, then cut the arc with a jigsaw or scroll saw.

STEP 7 Drill a ⅜"-diameter hole, centered on each leg, 7" up from the bottom edge. This hole prevents splitting of the legs once the relief cut is completed, which will draw the two halves tight. Use a jigsaw to make the relief cuts. Run the saw along a line that's centered on the leg, to the hole center.

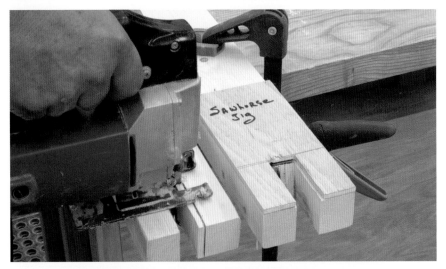

STEP 8 Cut a 1"-wide notch at the bottom of each leg. This notch should be centered on the leg and is 2½" long. Use a jigsaw to cut out the notch. The notch will allow the legs to fit in the foot dadoes. As shown, I've created a notch pattern jig for accurate and repetitive cuts.

STEP 9 This step is optional. If you have a router and ⅜"-radius roundover bit, ease all face corners. The roundover doesn't add anything to the sawhorses structurally, but the construction-grade lumber looks a little nicer.

STEP 10 Put the leg assembly on the feet and drill a ⅜"-diameter hole 1¼" up from each leg bottom. The hole will be drilled through both leg and foot. Thread a 4"-long carriage bolt through the hole and secure the assembly with a washer and wing nut. The bolt and nut will secure the foot to the leg, but can be easily removed for storage.

STEP 11 The final step is to drill a ⅜"-diameter hole at the halfway point on each leg to attach the feet for storage.

CONSTRUCTION
notes

As I mentioned, these sawhorses are worth a great deal more to me than the $5 cost to build them. However, if you want a better-looking unit, you can use any type of hardwood.

The height and width of these units are dimensions I decided would work best for my needs. You can change the width or height to suit your work by varying the legs and cross rail lengths. If you want a sawhorse that's almost impossible to tip over, lengthen the feet. They are, however, very steady with 20" feet.

The same design can be used to build extra-sturdy horses using 4x4 (3½" square) lumber. Lateral support rails can be attached to both sides of two saw-horses with a plywood top installed if you need a strong workbench that can be easily assembled on a job site. Or, four sawhorses supporting a 30"-wide by 96"-long sheet of ¾" plywood also make a great workbench.

Use wood dowels and glue to join the legs to the cross rails. If you'd rather not use dowels, two 1¼"-long screws, driven through each joint, will work just as well as long as the joint is glued.

Finally, an outdoor version of this saw-horse can be built using a weather-resistant wood and polyurethane adhesive. To further protect the horses outside, apply a couple of coats of paint.

Rolling Shop Cart

T he rolling shop cart is another must-have in my shop. I use it every day to move cut panels and lumber around the shop. It, and versions like it, continue to be just as valuable as my workbench.

My carts are normally made with low-cost construction-grade lumber. The top, middle and bottom shelves are inexpensive particleboard or plywood sheeting. They are often made with cut-offs and leftover panels that are on my wood rack. In fact, the only costly items are the metal wheel casters that I use to move the carts around the shop.

These carts are not restricted to a woodshop. I use mine when I have to work on my trailer or truck, because they are perfect tool trays. In the garage, these carts can be used as mobile workbenches for repairs around the home or as handy worktables for garden potting and planting. However, be warned, as soon as the gardener in your home spots this great three-shelf cart, you'll have to make another one for yourself.

I enjoy my power tools, but this rolling cart is more valuable than any tool I have when I have to move a dozen pieces of wood around the shop. I'm sure you'll appreciate its value after building one for your shop.

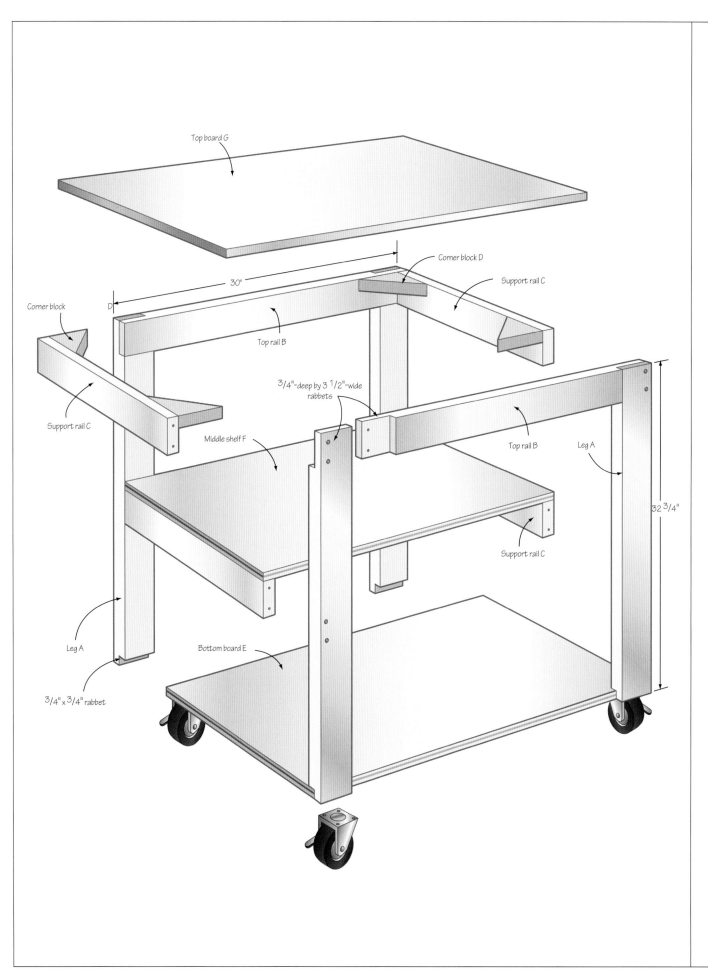

Top board G

Corner block D

Support rail C

30"

D

Top rail B

Corner block

Support rail C

3/4"-deep by 3 1/2"-wide rabbets

Middle shelf F

Top rail B

Leg A

Support rail C

32 3/4"

Leg A

Bottom board E

3/4" x 3/4" rabbet

Schedule of Materials: Rolling Shop Cart

LTR.	NO.	ITEM	STOCK	INCHES T	(MM) T	INCHES W	(MM) W	INCHES L	(MM) L	COMMENTS
A	4	legs	pine	1½	(38)	3½	(89)	32¾	(832)	
B	2	top rails	pine	1½	(38)	3½	(89)	30	(762)	
C	4	support rails	pine	1½	(38)	3½	(89)	21	(533)	
D	4	corner blocks	pine	3½	(89)	3½	(89)			angle cut at 45°
E	1	bottom board	particleboard	¾	(19)	22½	(572)	30	(762)	
F	1	middle shelf	particleboard	¾	(19)	21	(533)	30	(762)	
G	1	top board	particleboard	¾	(19)	26	(660)	32	(813)	

Supplies

¾" (19mm) Screws

1¼" (32mm) Screws

1½" (38mm) Screws

2" (51mm) Screws

3" (76mm) Screws

Nails

Glue

4   Wheel assemblies

STEP 1 I want the finished height of my cart to be 36", which is the same height as my workbench. The top is ¾" thick, and I'm using wheels that are 2½" high. The side frames should then be 32¾" high, and I'll build them 30" wide. Each of the four legs A requires a ¾"-wide by ¾"-deep rabbet on one end. These rabbets can be cut on a table saw using a standard blade by nibbling out the waste materials with multiple passes. If you have a dado blade, the rabbets can be cut very quickly.

STEP 2 Each top rail B needs a rabbet that's ¾" deep by 3½" wide on both ends. The legs A also need the same-size rabbet on the uncut ends. The larger top rabbet is cut on the same face as the rabbet on the opposite end. The larger rabbet cuts on the top rails and legs will form a half-lap joint.

STEP 3 The half-lap joint is secured with glue and 1¼"-long screws. Or you can use glue and wood dowels as detailed in project six for the sawhorses. Build the two frames using two legs and one top rail for each assembly. Be sure to apply wood glue to all surfaces of the rabbet cuts before clamping and securing with screws.

STEP 4 The frames can now be connected to each other using the support rails C. Two are at the top, flush with the top surface of the legs, and two are attached with their top edges 16" above the lower leg ends. Attach the rails to both frames with a simple butt joint and glue. Use two 3"-long screws, in pilot holes, to secure each joint. Corner blocks will strengthen these connections. Position the leg frames so the lower rabbet cuts on the legs face inward (or face each other).

STEP 5 Glue and nail the four corner blocks D in the top corners. They should be set flush with the top edge of the cart frame.

STEP 6 The bottom board E is a piece of ¾"-thick particleboard. Cut it to the size given in the materials list and install it in the ¾" rabbets at the bottom of each leg. Use glue and two 2"-long screws at each corner to secure this panel.

STEP 7 While the cart is upside down, attach the four wheel assemblies. I used a combination of ¾"- and 1½"-long screws to secure the wheels. The longer screws are positioned over the leg ends and are driven through the bottom board into the legs.

STEP 8 The middle shelf F is attached using four 2"-long screws. I don't want to use glue for this shelf, in case it has to be replaced in the future.

CONSTRUCTION
notes

This rolling cart is made using construction-grade framing lumber. If you want something a little better looking, use hardwood for the legs and rails. Be sure to counterbore the screw holes and fill them with wood plugs. You can always use mortise-and-tenon joints for the corner connections in place of the half-lap joints if you wish.

The finished height and width of your rolling cart should be tailored to your needs. My workbench is 36" high, but yours may not be, so change the cart height to match your bench. The cart width is fine for my shop, but you might want something different, so cut the support rails C shorter or longer to suit your needs.

My cart shelves are made of particleboard, however, plywood is stronger and can also be used. The wheels can be exchanged for heavy-duty models, along with plywood shelves to accommodate heavy loads. My shop floor is reasonably smooth concrete, but if it was rough I'd switch to a larger-diameter wheel.

My carts get bumped, bruised and beaten, which is why I use low-cost construction-grade lumber and particleboard shelves. The materials are inexpensive, so the carts can be rebuilt without spending a lot of money. However, even with the low-cost materials, these rolling carts are usable for five or six years in my shop.

STEP 9 The top board G is 2" wider and longer than the cart frame. That dimension will provide a 1" overhang on all edges. Attach the top with 2"-long screws through the corner blocks. Use a sander to round over the top board's corners to prevent injury.

Rolling Tool Cabinet

ome might say this cabinet project is a bit fancy for a shop tool cabinet. That's probably a true statement, but I have good reasons for building this frame and panel cabinet with oak. First, I had a lot of cutoff pieces in my shop, and this cabinetmaking style is the perfect way to use wood shorts. Second, and more importantly, I wanted to fully detail this building style for those who have never used frame and panel construction techniques.

This cabinetmaking style isn't just for shop cabinets; it can be used for a whole variety of projects in your home. Living room furniture, bedroom suites, sideboards, entertainment center cabinets and so on — it's an endless list. Before modern sheet goods became popular, frame and panel construction methods were widely used. You can easily build structural panels, doors, drawer faces or mirror frames once you understand this woodworking construction style.

I'll detail some of the other project options for the frame and panel style in the construction notes. However, look closely at the procedures used to create individual panels. That's the heart of this construction method — grooves and tenons. It sounds a bit complicated, but all that's involved is making basic saw cuts using a table saw. That's it! You can build all the panels and doors you need with your table saw and careful cutting. In fact, you don't even have to change the blade.

However, before you decide to tackle a house full of frame and panel cabinetry, build yourself this rolling tool cabinet. It's a great way to practice all the techniques, and you wind up with a useful and versatile shop cabinet.

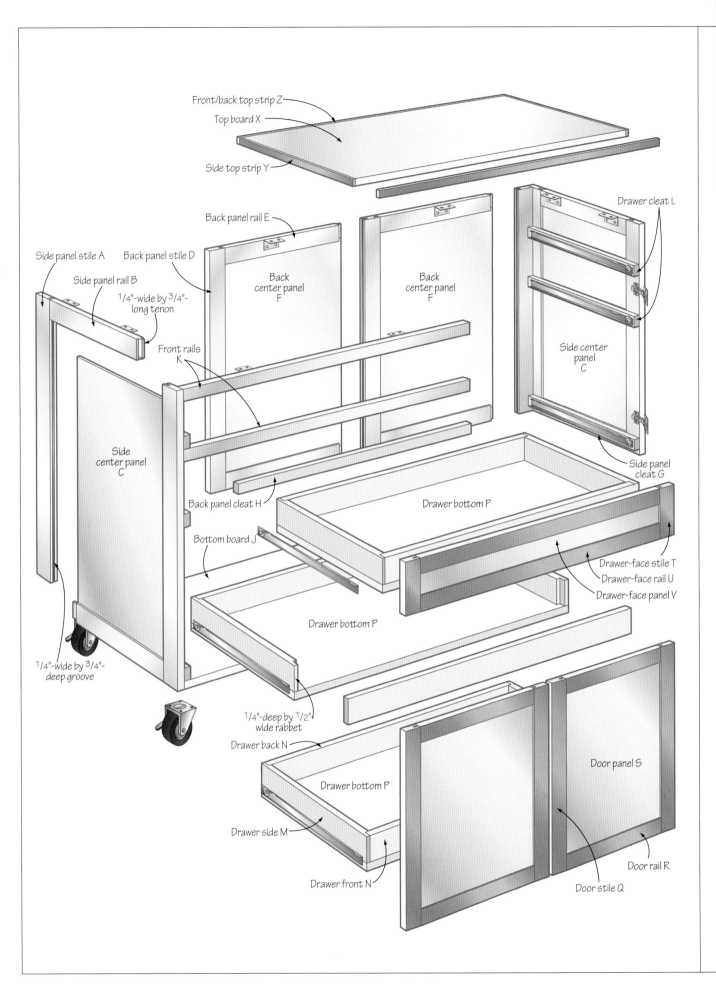

Front/back top strip Z

Top board X

Side top strip Y

Back panel rail E

Side panel stile A

Back panel stile D

Side panel rail B

1/4"-wide by 3/4"-long tenon

Back center panel F

Back center panel F

Drawer cleat L

Front rails K

Side center panel C

Side center panel C

Side panel cleat G

Back panel cleat H

Drawer bottom P

Bottom board J

Drawer bottom P

Drawer-face stile T

Drawer-face rail U

Drawer-face panel V

1/4"-wide by 3/4"-deep groove

1/4"-deep by 1/2"-wide rabbet

Drawer back N

Drawer bottom P

Door panel S

Drawer side M

Drawer front N

Door rail R

Door stile Q

Schedule of Materials: Rolling Tool Cabinet

LTR.	NO.	ITEM	STOCK	INCHES T	(MM) T	INCHES W	(MM) W	INCHES L	(MM) L
A	4	side panel stiles	hardwood	¾	(19)	2⅛	(54)	31	(787)
B	4	side panel rails	hardwood	¾	(19)	2⅛	(54)	17¼	(438)
C	2	side center panels	plywood	¼	(6)	17¼	(438)	28¼	(718)
D	3	back panel stiles	hardwood	¾	(19)	2⅛	(54)	31	(787)
E	4	back panel rails	hardwood	¾	(19)	2⅛	(54)	16⁵⁄₁₆	(414)
F	2	back center panels	plywood	¼	(6)	16⁵⁄₁₆	(414)	28¼	(718)
G	2	side panel cleats	hardwood	¾	(19)	1½	(38)	18½	(470)
H	1	back panel cleat	hardwood	¾	(19)	1½	(38)	36	(914)
J	1	bottom board	plywood	¾	(19)	19¼	(489)	36	(914)
K	2	front rails	hardwood	¾	(19)	1½	(38)	36	(914)
L	4	drawer cleats	hardwood	¾	(19)	1½	(38)	19	(483)
M	6	drawer sides	plywood	½	(13)	3½	(89)	18	(457)
N	6	drawer fronts and backs	plywood	½	(13)	3½	(89)	33	(838)
P	3	drawer bottoms	plywood	½	(13)	18	(457)	33½	(851)
Q	4	door stiles	hardwood	¾	(19)	2⅛	(54)	23½	(597)
R	4	door rails	hardwood	¾	(19)	2⅛	(54)	15¾	(400)
S	2	door panels	plywood	¼	(6)	15¾	(400)	20¾	(527)
T	2	drawer-face stiles	hardwood	¾	(19)	2⅛	(54)	6	(152)
U	2	drawer-face rails	hardwood	¾	(19)	2⅛	(54)	34¼	(870)
V	1	drawer-face panel	plywood	¼	(6)	3¼	(83)	34¼	(870)
W	1	drawer-face filler	plywood	¼	(6)	1¾	(45)	30	(762)
X	1	top board	plywood	¾	(19)	23	(584)	39	(991)
Y	2	side top strips	hardwood	¼	(6)	¾	(19)	23	(584)
Z	2	front/back top strips	hardwood	¼	(6)	¾	(19)	39½	(1003)
AA	1	bottom strip	hardwood	¼	(6)	¾	(19)	39½	(1003)

Supplies

Glue

Brad nails

Colored putty

8 Right-angle brackets

4 Wheels

4 European-style hidden hinges and plates

3 18" (457mm) Full-extension drawer glide sets

3 Handles

⁵⁄₁₆" (8mm) Lag screws

⁵⁄₁₆" (8mm) or ⅜" (10mm) Bolts, nuts and washers

Wood plugs

1½" (38mm) Screws

1¼" (32mm) Screws

1" (25 mm) Screws

⅝" (16mm) Screws

SHOP tip

STEP 1 Cut the side panel stiles A and rails B to the sizes indicated in the materials list. Form a ¼"-wide by ¾"-deep groove (see shop tip before cutting) in the center of all stiles and rails. The side center panels C will fit into the grooves. To cut the grooves, set your table saw fence ¼" away from the blade, which should be ¾" above the table's top surface. Run one side edge of each board through the saw, then reverse the boards so the opposite face of each board is against the fence. Push the boards through again. This technique will center each groove on the edges of all stiles and rails. Depending on the saw blade width (kerf), you may have to run each board through the blade at the center of each groove to clean the channel.

STEP 2 The rails require a ¾"-long by ¼"-thick (or equal to the groove width) tenon on both ends. The tenons will fit into the grooves in the stiles. You can form the tenons in a number of ways, but always be sure to cut test pieces for a trial fit. Set the outside face of the blade ¾" away from the saw fence. Nibble away with multiple cuts using the miter slide on each face of the rail to form the tenons (top photo). Use a tenon-cutting jig if you have one available. On each face of the rail you'll need to make a shoulder cut that's ¾" from the end, before removing the waste material. Install a dado blade and fence to form the tenons (top, right photo). The stacked dado blade is a little expensive, but a good carbide-tipped set is a useful addition to any woodworking shop. It's normally adjustable from ⅛" to ¹³⁄₁₆" and will be used on many of your woodworking projects. You can cut rabbets, grooves or dadoes quickly, easily and accurately with this blade (photo at right).

STEP 3 Cut the center panels C for each side frame. Assemble the rails and stiles around each panel by inserting the panel and the rail tenons into the grooves. When you are sure everything fits together correctly, apply glue on the tenons and clamp until the adhesive sets. You can check the frame for square by measuring both diagonals on each assembly (see photo in step 14). Adjust if necessary by tapping lightly on the long side until both measurements are equal.

STEP 4 The back panel is 36" wide, so three back panel stiles D will be installed for added strength. Cut the stiles D and rails E to size, then form the grooves and tenons as in steps 1 and 2. One of the stiles D, which should be marked as the center stile, requires a groove on each long edge to receive the panels and rail tenons. Dry fit all the parts before starting the final assembly with the center panels.

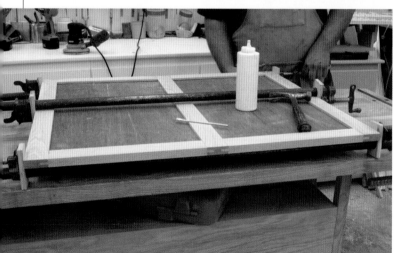

STEP 5 Prepare the two back center panels F and assemble the back frame. Use glue on the tenons and clamp the assembly until the adhesive sets.

STEP 6 Before attaching the two side panels to the back; install the bottom support cleats G and H. The cleats are set ¾" above the bottom edge of each panel and secured with glue and 1¼"-long screws. The two on the side panels are aligned flush with the side panel's front edges, leaving a 1½" space at the back end of each panel. At this point you will have a right- and left-side panel. These cleats serve a number of purposes. They strengthen each panel, support the bottom board, provide a solid surface to attach the drawer glide hardware and properly space the pullouts to clear the door edges.

STEP 7 Join the side panels to the back panel with glue and 1½"-long screws. Counterbore the screw pilot holes so they can be filled with wood plugs and sanded smooth. Five screws in each corner will secure the panels, but space them evenly as the wood plugs will be visible. The cabinet should measure 37½" wide on the back face.

STEP 8 The bottom is a ¾"-thick piece of oak veneer plywood with a ¼"-thick strip of hardwood on the front edge. Attach the bottom strip AA to the bottom board J with glue and brad nails, then use a colored putty to fill the nail holes. Secure the bottom board to the three cleats G and H with glue and 1½"-long screws.

STEP 9 The upper and lower front rails K strengthen the cabinet, define the drawer box space and provide an upper center stop for the doors. The upper rail is installed flush with the side panels' top edges. Leave a 5" space between the two rails for the drawer box. Secure each rail end with two 1½"-long screws in counterbored holes that can be filled with ⅜"-diameter wood plugs.

STEP 10 The two upper drawers also need cleats L to support the glide hardware. The bottom edges of the top drawer's cleats are installed in line with the top edge of the lower rail. The middle drawer's cleats can be installed in any position, so allow enough space between the two bottom drawers to suit your tool storage requirements. I've aligned my cleats to have a 16" space above the bottom board. That position will let me use the lowest drawer for tall power tools like circular saws. Fasten the cleats using glue and 1¼"-long screws into the front and back stiles of the side panels.

STEP 11 Generally, drawer boxes are 1" less in height and width than the drawer opening, when using standard drawer glide hardware like the 18" full-extension glides I'm using. That rule can be used with almost all drawer glides, but check the specifications with your hardware before building the boxes. To simplify cutting, I will make all my drawer boxes the same size. Each drawer box will be 4" high and 33½" wide. I'm using ½"-thick Baltic birch plywood for the drawer boxes, which is a favorite material with many cabinetmakers. Each drawer side has a ¼"-deep by ½"-wide rabbet on both ends to accept the fronts and backs N. Cut the parts to size using the same techniques that you used to cut the rail tenons.

STEP 12 The drawers are assembled using glue and brad nails. Apply glue to the rabbet cuts and attach the side boards to the front and back boards. The drawer bottom P is also attached with glue and brads.

STEP 13 Install the drawer glide hardware onto the cleats G and L, following the manufacturer's instructions. Most glide hardware, as mentioned earlier, needs ½" clearance on each side of the drawer box. I'm using full-extension (FX) glides, but a standard three-quarter-extension glide will work just as well.

STEP 14 The doors are made following the same steps as the side panels. My doors are flush with the bottom edge of the cabinet and overlay the middle rail by ½". The total door height is 23½". When two doors are to be installed using European-style hidden hinges, door width is determined by adding 1" to the cabinet's interior dimension and dividing by two. The interior width of the cabinet is 36". Adding 1" and dividing by two means I'll need two 18½"-wide doors to properly fit on the cabinet. Cut all the door parts Q, R and S and construct both doors. Measure the diagonals to ensure the doors are square.

STEP 15 The drawer face is also built using frame and panel construction techniques. It's typically 1" wider than the inside cabinet width and 1" higher than the drawer space opening height. Using those guidelines, the drawer face will be 6" high and 37" wide. Using parts T, U and V, build the drawer face following the same assembly procedures as the doors.

STEP 16 The doors will be mounted using European-style hidden hinges. I'm using full-overlay 107° hinges and standard side plates. Each door needs two 35mm-diameter holes for the hinges. The holes are 4" on center from each end and drilled ⅛" away from the door edge. I recommend that you purchase a small, inexpensive drill press to make the hinge holes. This is one procedure that's difficult to do without a drill press.

STEP 17 Attach the hinges to the doors with ⅝"-long screws. Use a square to be sure the hinge arm is 90° to the door edge.

STEP 19 The drawer face is attached to the box with four 1"-long screws driven through the front board and into the back of the drawer face. But first, cut the drawer-face filler W and tape it to the back of the drawer's center panel. This will prevent the drawer handle from bending the center panel. Any scrap piece of ¼"-thick material will work fine.

STEP 18 Connect the plates to the hinges and hold the door in its normally open position on the cabinet with a ⅛"-thick spacer between the cabinet and door. Drive ⅝"-long screws through the hinge plate holes and into the side panel stiles to anchor the hinge plates. The doors will be accurately aligned using this simple installation procedure.

STEP 20 Secure the drawer face to the box so the face is centered on the drawer opening.

STEP 21 Install single or double metal right-angle brackets to secure the top board.

STEP 22 A number of styles and materials can be used for the tool cabinet top. I discuss some of the options in the construction notes. However, for my use, a plywood veneer top will work fine. The top board X is edged with ¼" hardwood strips Y and Z. You can cut the strips on a table saw, or purchase a suitable stock moulding at the lumber store. The strips are attached with glue and brad nails. The overall top size is 23½" x 39½".

STEP 23 The top is secured to the cabinet with ⅝"-long screws in the right-angle brackets. I've set my top board to have a 1" overhang on each side and 1½" overhang on the front and back face of the cabinet.

STEP 24 I've installed four heavy-duty locking wheels to my cabinet. The locking feature will be handy when I want to use the cabinet as a table saw extension or mobile workbench or for a small power tool like a grinder. Use ⁵⁄₁₆" lag screws, driven into the lower cleats, to secure the wheels. If the holes are not located under the cleats, use ⁵⁄₁₆"- or ⅜"-diameter bolts, nuts and washers. Once the fit and operation of the drawers is checked and completed, apply a finish to the cabinet. I used three coats of polyurethane to finish the cabinet then installed door and drawer handles.

CONSTRUCTION
notes

The most important construction issue is the process of building frame and panel cabinetry, not the type of wood you use. You might want to use a lower-priced wood that can be painted or a different species that's readily available and less expensive in your area.

The purpose of this project is to practice frame and panel construction. This cabinetry style can be used to build dozens of furniture pieces for your home. Projects like entertainment centers, bedroom furniture, portable bars, cabinet doors and display cabinets can be built using frames and panels.

I used G1S (good one side) ¼" veneer plywood for my center panels because I wasn't concerned about the cabinet's interior appearance. However, the inside can be as beautiful as the outside by using G2S (good two sides) veneer plywood.

If this rolling tool cabinet will be used as a woodworking tool bench, a plywood top will be fine. But you might want to use it in the garage to work on your car or lawnmower. If that is your situation, a laminate top or possibly a metal cover for the top board would be more suitable.

Locks can be installed on the doors and drawer box. Good drawer locks are available at your local home-improvement store. One of the doors can be fastened with barrel bolts, but you'll have to set back the bottom drawer. The barrel bolts can be slid into a hole in the middle rail and in the bottom board. Then the other door can be locked to the fixed door, which should provide enough security to keep your tools tucked safely away.

However, the main focus of this project is frame and panel construction. Take your time and practice the techniques because you can use this woodworking style for hundreds of applications. And best of all, the panels can be made with any low-cost table saw, proving once again that you don't need a fortune in tools to build great furniture!

Tall Storage Cabinets

Your workshop might be in a garage that you share with the family car, or in a basement, or you may be lucky enough to have a dedicated woodworking shop. However, all shops share a common problem — not enough storage space for those hundreds of small items and tools.

We have screws, nails, glues, cleaners, stains and finishes, dowels, biscuits and so on. It's a never-ending list of items that we need for our projects, but finding a particular item when we need it can sometimes be a real challenge. How many times have you said, "Now where did I put those handles?" These cabinets may be just the solution you need to organize your shop.

Once again, don't spend time thinking about my choice of sheet material. That's not as important as the construction procedures, which will be the same no matter what you use. I'll discuss some material and hardware options as the project is built and suggest alternatives in the construction notes at the end of the project. The important issues to consider are the cabinet's size, how many shelves you'll need, the adjustable feature of these shelves and the level of security you require. If you plan to store paints and stains in these cabinets versus hardware, you may want to install a lock on the doors.

I built two cabinets to illustrate the versatility of this design; however, you may need a different size, so look at your requirements before cutting the panels. I'll also show you how to lay out a sheet-cutting diagram, which you should do with every project to save time and materials. This is the process I go through for everything I build, and it

helps me analyze my design.

I enjoy building these storage cabinets and really appreciate how they help organize a shop. These two were put to good use at my friend's auto repair shop. They help eliminate the frustration of time wasted looking for parts and sup-

plies. I'm sure you, too, will understand how valuable these cabinets are after you begin using them in your workshop. Remember, analyze your storage requirements before beginning, because those needs determine the cabinet sizes.

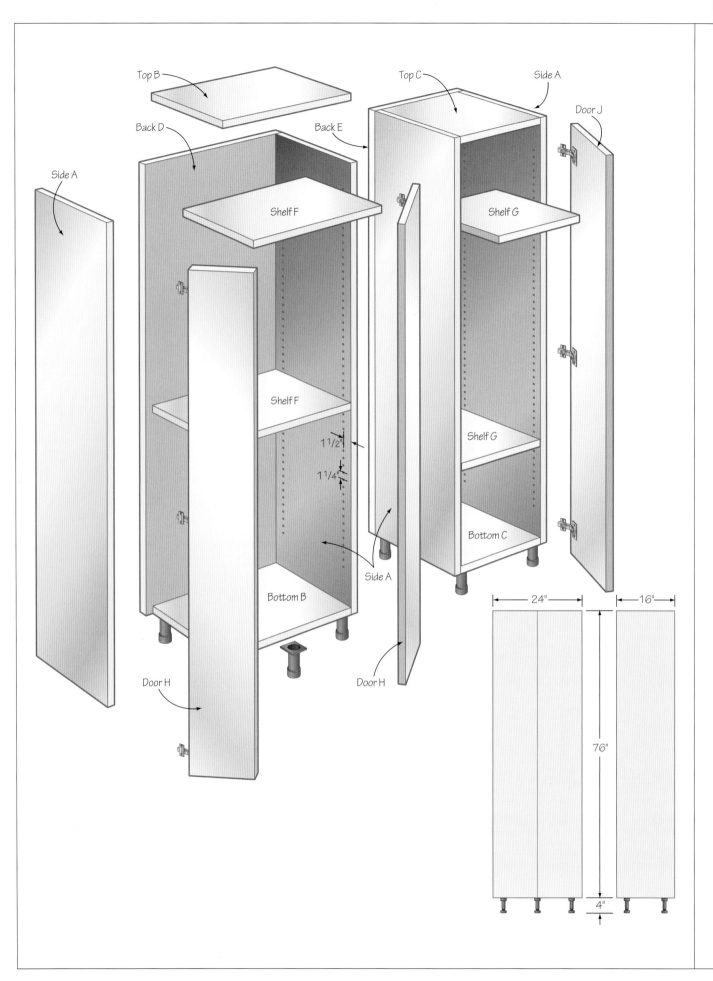

Top B

Side A

Back D

Back E

Top C

Side A

Door J

Shelf F

Shelf G

Shelf F

1 1/2"

1 1/4"

Shelf G

Side A

Bottom C

Bottom B

Door H

Door H

24"

16"

76"

4"

Schedule of Materials: Tall Storage Cabinets

LTR.	NO.	ITEM	STOCK	INCHES T	(MM) T	INCHES W	(MM) W	INCHES L	(MM) L	SHEET LAYOUT IDENTIFIERS
A	4	sides	MDF	¾	(19)	15¼	(387)	76	(1930)	1,2,3,4
B	2	top and bottom	MDF	¾	(19)	15¼	(387)	22½	(572)	5,6
C	2	top and bottom	MDF	¾	(19)	15¼	(387)	14½	(368)	7,8
D	1	back	MDF	¾	(19)	24	(610)	76	(1930)	9
E	1	back	MDF	¾	(19)	16	(406)	76	(1930)	10
F	6	shelves	MDF	¾	(19)	15¼	(387)	22⁷⁄₁₆	(570)	11,12,13,14,15,16
G	6	shelves	MDF	¾	(19)	15¼	(387)	14⁷⁄₁₆	(367)	17,18,19,20,21,22
H	2	doors	MDF	¾	(19)	11¾	(298)	76	(1930)	23,24
J	1	door	MDF	¾	(19)	15½	(394)	76	(1930)	25

Supplies

10 Cabinet legs

9   107° Hinges and plates

3   Handles

1½" (38mm) Particleboard screws

⅝" (16mm) Screws

Glue

48 Shelf pins

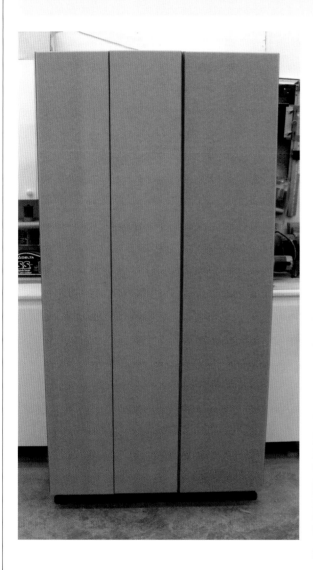

STEP 1 Before cutting the panels for any woodworking project, you should draw a sheet layout plan as shown in the illustration. Sizes are detailed, and a unique number is assigned to each part for easy identification. This step eliminates material waste and reduces errors. Review the drawing and notice the numerical identifiers on the panels. As you draw the sheets, try to group the rip sizes and crosscutting dimensions. If you plan to do a lot of projects and like the sheet layout process, you'll find a number of reasonably priced programs on the Internet. I use a software package called CutList Plus from www.cutlistplus.com.

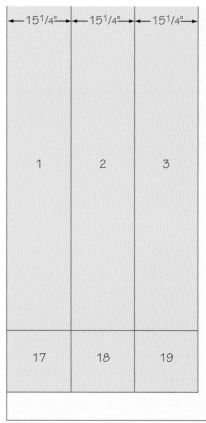

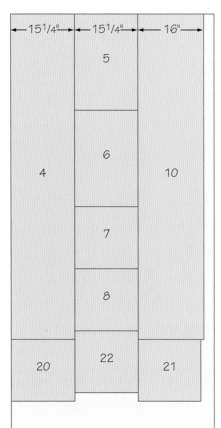

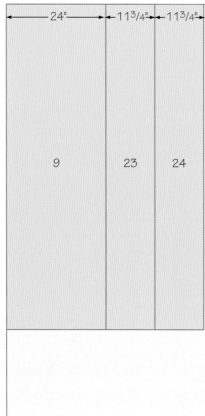

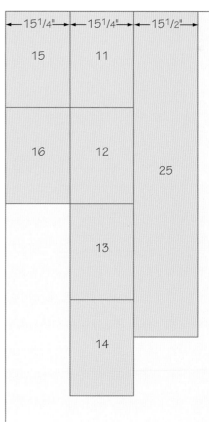

SHOP tip

I found almost no MDF panel splitting when I used 1½"-long screws compared to the 2" screws. Keep the screws at least 1" away from the board ends and cover the edges with glue. A combination of 1½"-long particleboard screws, in drilled pilot holes with glue added, seems to be the best procedure for a strong joint.

STEP 2 Cut all the panels to the sizes shown in the materials list. Review the sheet layout diagram for cutting patterns. These panels can be cut on a table saw or with a circular saw, or ripped to size by the lumberyard for a small fee. Write the panel identifier number on a nonvisible edge of each panel. Indicate the top end of each side panel so they can be positioned correctly when you drill the shelf pin holes. Numbering each panel eliminates the need to measure and hunt through a pile of cut parts trying to find the correct piece.

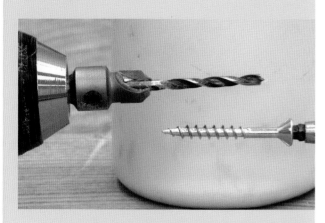

STEP 3 Drill one face of each side panel A with a bit to match the diameter of the shelf pins you plan to use. My holes are spaced about 1¼" apart and 1½" in from the front and back edges. Build a drilling jig, as shown in the photo, and place a wood dowel on the drill bit to limit the depth of each hole. Be sure to start the holes at the top of each side panel so they will be correctly aligned on each panel. I always try to use the numbered end of my panels as the top edge, to eliminate drilling and assembly mistakes.

STEP 4 Join the sides A of each case to the top and bottom boards B and C. Assemble both the 16"- and 24"-wide cases. Use glue and 1½" particleboard screws (see shop tip) for the assembly. Four screws per connection, along with yellow carpenter's glue, will form a strong joint.

STEP 5 The backs D and E are the full height and width of each cabinet. Attach them with glue and 1½"-long screws in piloted holes that are about 8" apart.

STEP 6 Both cabinets will have plastic adjustable legs installed. Moisture and shop liquids do not affect plastic legs, so they are an ideal choice for workshop cabinets. These legs don't have a great deal of side strength, so dragging the cabinet across a floor can snap one easily. However, they have a 650-pound load rating, so they can hold just about anything you plan to store in the cabinets. The 16"-wide case has four legs, and the 24"-wide unit will have six legs. I've installed two legs in the center of the wider 24" cabinet for added support. Set the front legs 2" back from the cabinet's front edge for kick space. Position the back legs at the edge and back so the leg flange is under the side and back panel edges. The cabinet load will be transferred from the shelves to the side panels, then to the legs and finally the floor.

STEP 7 Door sizes are based on interior cabinet widths, and the rule states that the door is 1" wider than the cabinet's inside dimension. If you need two doors, then simply take that inside width dimension plus 1", and divide by 2 to find the exact width of each door. This is a frameless-style tall cabinet, so the door height equals the cabinet height. If you have access to a small router and ⅜" roundover bit, ease the outside face of each door H and J to soften the look. However, each door can just as easily stay a square, flat panel.

STEP 8 Drill three 35mm-diameter hinge holes in each door for the 107° hidden hinges. Two of the holes on the doors can be located 7" from each end, and the third should be located halfway between them. Each hole is drilled ⅛" away from the door edge.

STEP 9 Attach the hinges to the door in the 35mm-diameter holes. The hinge arms should be 90° to the door's edge, so use a square to align the hinges. Use ⅝"-long screws to secure the hinges.

CONSTRUCTION
notes

Once all the doors are hung, install the handles. When you are satisfied that all the shelves fit and the doors work properly, remove the hardware and paint the cabinets. A good primer and one or two coats of paint will properly finish and protect your cabinets.

Someone asked why I didn't use one door on the 24"-wide cabinet. I did consider doing that, but a sheet of ¾"-thick MDF weighs about 90 pounds, so a 23½"-wide door would weigh 30 to 35 pounds, and that would be quite a load for the hinges. I believe there will be less strain and longer hinge life with the two-door setup.

Use any type of sheet material you prefer to build these storage cabinets. I like MDF because it's inexpensive and won't be subjected to any moisture in my application. However, plywood, particleboard or just about any other ¾"-thick sheet material can be used. It's your choice. The building procedure, not the material, is most important for this project.

If you can, purchase metal shelf pins for maximum support so you won't have to worry about overloading the shelves. These cabinets can be fitted with padlocks to keep children safe from the harmful chemicals that we sometimes use. The two-door cabinet can have a padlock installed as long as one door is secured on the inside with barrel bolts. Drill holes for the barrel in the top and bottom boards, then install the hasp on the opposite door.

If you haven't got a ready supply of plastic legs in your area, a fixed base can be used. But the legs make leveling a lot quicker, so it is worth looking for a local or mail-order supplier. They normally cost between $1 and $2 per leg.

Four sheets of MDF with hardware and legs cost less than $150 and build two great storage cabinets. That's a small price for a lot of organization in my friend's shop!

STEP 10 Doors can be accurately and easily attached to the cabinets. First, attach the hinge plates to the hinge bodies and place blocks under one corner of the cabinet to support the door so that its bottom edge is aligned with the underside of the cabinet's bottom board. Place a ⅛"-thick spacer between the cabinet and door while holding the door in its normally open position. The hinge plates will then be properly located. Drive ⅝"-long screws through the plate holes and into the cabinet side. The doors will be accurately and securely mounted once all the hinge plate screws are installed.

Hand Tool Wall Cabinet

I believe every shop should have a dedicated wall cabinet for hand tools. Your woodworking shop might be in a garage or the basement of your home, or you may be lucky enough to have a separate shop built on your property. The physical layout doesn't matter, because we all have planes, chisels, turning tools or carving knives that should be protected from dust and dirt.

Many of us store these tools on open shelving, so they are usually scattered all over the shop. When they require cleaning and sharpening we have to hunt and gather these tools, along with our sharpening equipment, which is a waste of valuable shop time. Why not keep all these tools in one cabinet with doors, which will extend their useful service as well as reduce the time required to maintain them? This project will address those needs and, as an added bonus, show you how to build cabinet doors with acrylic center panels so everyone can see these wonderful tools.

I do not like using glass for door panels in a workshop. A flying piece of wood from a machine, or a long board being carried into the shop can easily break the glass and cause a serious accident. Acrylics, sometimes referred to by trade names such as Plexiglas, are the answer because they won't shatter when hit.

This project will show you more about dado blade usage on a table saw. And if you plan to buy one accessory in the near future, a carbide-tipped stacked dado blade set is one of the best investments you can make. It will double the usefulness of your saw because you'll be able to quickly and accurately cut

dadoes, grooves and rabbet joints as well as tenons and finger joints. I'll also show you how to make another valuable accessory for your saw that will let you crosscut long boards with increased safety. This crosscutting panel jig can be made for less than $10, but you'll soon discover its true value.

This cabinet will be used to store hand tools and water baths with stones.

However, it isn't limited to that particular use. A wood carver could use it for small carving tools; a scroll saw enthusiast may want to store small patterns and jigs; or you might simply need a dedicated storage area for drill, shaper and router bits. When you need safe, easily accessible, relatively dust-free storage with easy-to-see-through doors, this is the cabinet for your shop.

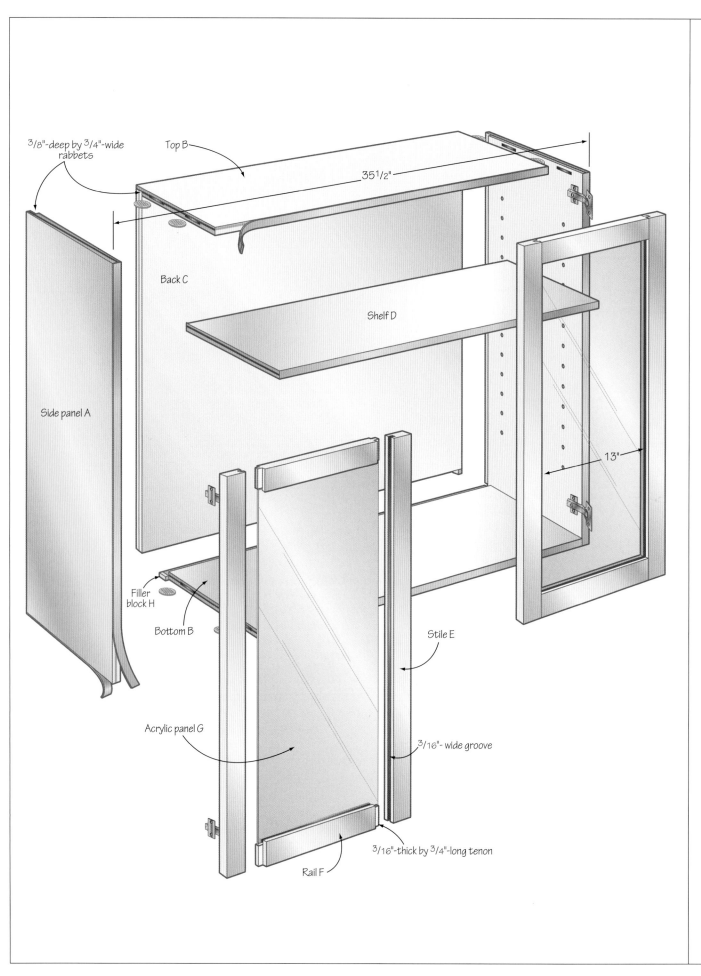

3/8"-deep by 3/4"-wide rabbets

Top B

35 1/2"

Back C

Shelf D

Side panel A

13"

Filler block H

Bottom B

Stile E

Acrylic panel G

3/16"- wide groove

3/16"-thick by 3/4"-long tenon

Rail F

Schedule of Materials: Hand Tool Wall Cabinet

LTR.	NO.	ITEM	STOCK	INCHES T	(MM) T	INCHES W	(MM) W	INCHES L	(MM) L
A	2	side panels	veneer ply	¾	(19)	12	(305)	27	(686)
B	2	top and bottom	veneer ply	¾	(19)	12	(305)	34	(864)
C	1	back	veneer ply	¾	(19)	26¼	(667)	34¾	(883)
D	2	shelves	veneer ply	¾	(19)	11¼	(286)	33¹⁵⁄₁₆	(862)
E	4	stiles	hardwood	¾	(19)	2¼	(57)	27	(686)
F	4	rails	hardwood	¾	(19)	2¼	(57)	14½	(368)
G	2	panels	acrylic	⅛	(3)	14½	(368)	24	(610)
H		filler block							

Supplies

Glue

Finishing nails

No. 20 biscuits

4 European-style hidden hinges and plates

Wood-veneer edge tape

8 Handles

8 ⅝" (16mm) Ccrews

Shelf pins

SHOP tip

Some wood edge tapes are difficult to trim with a knife because the cut tends to follow the grain pattern. If you have a router and flush-trim bit with a bearing guide, use that method. If not, use a very sharp knife and trim the edges smooth.

STEP 1 Before you begin, refer to the end of this chapter and read the sidebar called "Making a Crosscutting Panel Jig." You can build this inexpensive jig for your table saw to safely crosscut the long ripped panels for the cabinet case.

STEP 2 Cut the side panels A and top and bottom B for the wall cabinet cases. Apply wood-veneer edge tape (to match the sheet material you are using) to the front (one long edge) of each panel. I'm using a preglued iron-on wood-veneer tape.

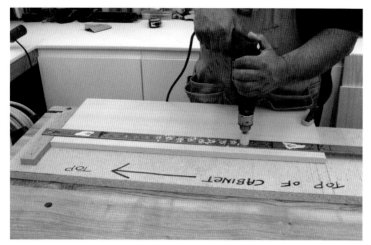

STEP 3 Drill two columns of holes in each side panel A. The hole diameter should match your choice of shelf pins. The hole columns are about 2" in from each long edge and spaced about 1½" apart. Remember to start the holes from the top edge of each side panel and on each inside face so the wood-veneer taped edges are facing in the same direction. You can easily drill the holes using the jig shown. The jig is simply a flat piece of metal with evenly spaced drilled holes and stop supports at each end. I have a wood dowel rod on the bit to limit the hole depth.

STEP 4 Before you start to assemble the case, cut a ⅜"-deep by ¾"-w rabbet on the inside back face of each side panel A and top and bott B. A router or dado blade on your table saw will easily cut the plywoo veneer panels.

STEP 5 The two side panels A can be rabbeted on both ends and joined to the top and bottom B with glue, then clamped until the adhesive sets. Or you can use glue and finishing nails to secure the bottom and top boards in the side panel end rabbets if you don't have long clamps. However, I'm using butt joinery and biscuits to assemble my case. If you have a biscuit joiner, you might want to consider this method for your cabinet. Cut biscuit slots at the 3" and 9" marks, measured from each front edge, on each panel. Put glue on the edges and in the biscuit slots, insert No. 20 biscuits and clamp the case until the adhesive sets.

STEP 6 Cut the back C, apply glue to the rabbet cuts and set the panel in place. Use finishing nails to secure the panel so the glue will properly set up.

STEP 7 Fill the rabbet cuts on the bottom of the cabinet with small filler blocks H. Use glue to secure these fillers and sand flush when the adhesive sets. They will provide a flat surface for the wood-veneer edge tape that will be applied to cover the lower end cuts of the side boards.

STEP 8 Cut the two shelves D to the size noted in the materials list. Apply wood-veneer edge tape to the front edge of each shelf. While your iron is hot, put edge tape on the bottom (visible) ends of each side panel A. The top ends of the side panels won't be seen, so they don't need to be covered.

STEP 9 The doors are at the full cabinet height of 27", which is typical with frameless-style upper cabinets. The door width, using European-style hidden hinges, is 1" greater than the inside cabinet dimension of 34". If you require two doors, which is the case with this cabinet, divide the inside dimension of 34" plus 1", by two. Therefore, the cabinet will need two doors 17½" wide by 27" high. All stiles (vertical members) and rails (horizontal members) are 2¼" wide. Prepare all the door parts (stiles E and rails F), remembering that the 14½" length of each rail includes material to cut ¾"-long tenons on each end. Each of the eight door members requires a ¾"-deep by 3⁄16"-wide groove on one long edge. The groove will hold the rail tenons and the 1⁄8"-thick acrylic center panel G.

STEP 10 The tenon on both ends of the four rails is 3⁄16" thick by ¾" long. It can be cut by making multiple passes over a standard table saw blade or in one pass using a stacked dado blade set on your table saw.

STEP 11 The door frames can now be partially assembled for other machine work and finishing at this point. Glue and clamp one rail to the stiles. Dry fit the other rail because it will be removed later to install the acrylic center panel. Use a 3⁄8" roundover bit in your router to soften the outside perimeter of each door frame. Once the machine work is complete, apply a finish to the cabinet and door frames.

SHOP tip

The grooves on all the rails and stiles are ³⁄₁₆" wide, and the acrylic panels I'm using are ⅛" thick. The added ³⁄₁₆" of groove width will allow the panels to float so the stiles and rails can expand and contract with seasonal changes.

STEP 12 Once your finish has dried, remove the nonglued rail and install the acrylic panel G in each door. Apply glue to the rail tenons and clamp the frames until the adhesive cures.

STEP 13 Install two 100° to 120° hinges on each door, in 35mm-diameter hinge holes. Drill the hinge holes about 4" from each door end and ⅛" away from the door edge. Use ⅝" screws to secure the hinges, making sure they are at right angles to the door edge.

STEP 14 Clip the hinge plate on the hinges and install the doors on the cabinet. Hold the door in its normally open position on the cabinet, with a ⅛" spacer between the door and cabinet side panel edge. Drive ⅝" screws through the hinge plate holes into the cabinet side. The doors will be properly mounted and aligned using this simple technique. Install the door handles to complete the cabinet.

Making a Crosscutting Panel Jig

STEP 1 Cut a piece of ¾"-thick sheet material that's approximately 24" wide by 36" long. You'll also need a strip of hardwood that fits snugly, without binding, in one of the miter slots on your table saw. The hardwood strip should be about 30" long, so a few inches of the material will extend past the front and rear edges of the sheet material. Most miter slots are ¾" wide and about ¼" to ⅜" deep. Attach the hardwood strip to the bottom face of the panel, parallel to one 24"-long edge. Draw a line parallel to the panel's edge to guide the strip placement, being sure to mark it so that 1" of panel extends past the blade.

STEP 2 Place the panel, with the hardwood strip attached, in the miter slot and cut the panel overhang. This cut will align the panel travel parallel to the saw blade.

STEP 3 Use a carpenter's framing square to align a 1½"-wide by ¾"-thick hardwood guide at 90° to the panel's cut edge. Panels are to be cut crest against the hardwood guide and pushed through the saw blade on the panel jig. Secure the guide with screws.

CONSTRUCTION
notes

I've used acrylic for my center panels, but you can use plywood veneer or glass. However, for safety reasons I would not use glass panel doors in a workshop, and I strongly suggest you don't, either. The acrylic sheets are inexpensive and will not shatter if something strikes them. If you do decide to use glass, make sure it is tempered, so it will not shatter if broken.

My cabinet is about 35½" wide by 27" high, because that size meets my requirements. However, the cabinet can be any size using the same construction steps. I've used wood shelves, but ¼"-thick acrylic can also be used for the shelving if you want to install a light in the cabinet to illuminate the interior. The cabinet depth is also variable should you want to store bigger equipment. The size doesn't matter — it's the building steps that are important.

How would you join your cabinet box? As earlier suggested, you might want to cut side panel end rabbets and use glue, or you might want to use screws and glue. Also, the cabinet back can be overlapped instead of inset in the rabbets. A ¼"-thick sheet of veneer plywood might also be an option for your back panel.

I've used oak veneer plywood to build my cabinet and sprayed three coats of lacquer on all wood surfaces. However, your can use almost any sheet material, such as melamine particleboard or plywood, and paint the cabinet. If cost is an issue, use ¾" particleboard or MDF for the cabinet carcass and doors, then apply a couple coats of oil-based paint to all surfaces.

The doors can be made of sheet material if you don't need to see the cabinet interior. Install a latch on one door and padlock hasp on the front if you need a secure cabinet for expensive tools, or one that you don't want accessible to children. You can build a few of these cabinets using melamine particleboard, as I have in my shop, with solid, flat panel melamine doors for tool and hardware storage. Most of the cabinets in my shop are white melamine to reflect as much light as possible and maximize my storage.

And finally, don't limit this cabinet construction method as shop storage only. This design can be used anywhere in your home. How about upper cabinets over the washer and dryer, wall cabinets in the children's room for toys and books, added storage for your home office or possibly a few nice wall cabinets with glass panels for the kitchen?

Power Miter Saw Station

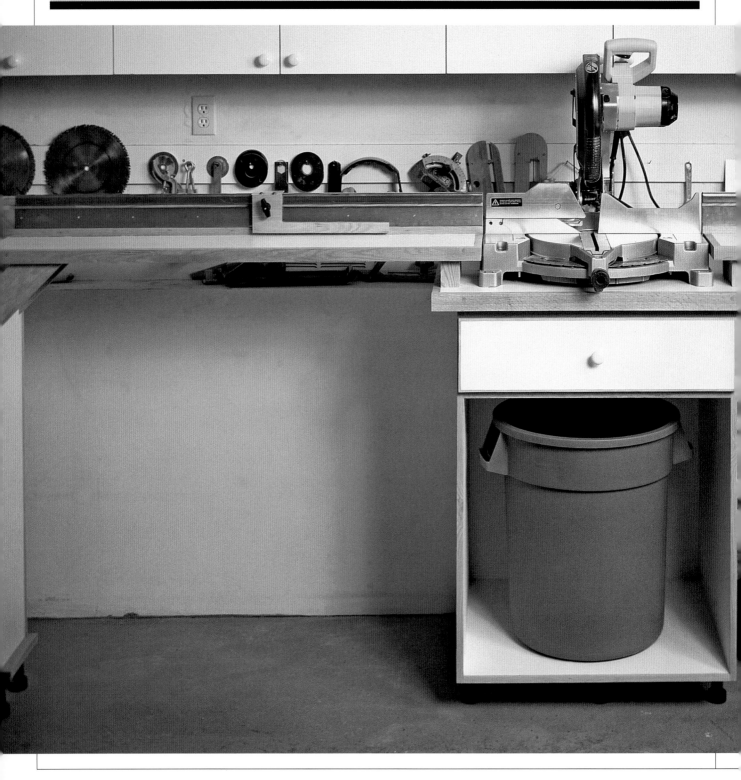

I wanted to meet a number of requirements when I designed my ultimate power miter saw station.

First, the station tower had to be wide enough so I could tuck a large garbage pail inside. It also had to have easy access so I could clear and throw away scraps of wood. I sometimes get lazy and forget to remove the small scraps of wood after cutting. These pieces can contact the blade on the next cut and shoot out of the saw like a wild bullet. I have seen too many close calls using this saw, so this design feature was high on my list.

I also wanted the station fences or "wings" on my station to be high enough so I could use the floor space; I will be storing rolling workstations under the saw fences. My table height is 42" off the ground and the fences are about 2½" higher.

The station tower has a drawer to store wrenches, instruction books and any other saw accessories. I usually spend time searching the shop for these items, so I promised myself they would have a place in the station.

I was tired of using poorly designed stop blocks that could be used only for material cuts starting at 6" or more. Why couldn't a zero stop be made? I think that need was met with my stop-block system.

Finally, the "wings" had to be strong because they would be 4' to 8' long without a center support. I used hardwood and steel to edge the sheet material and make the stop-block system. The fences are extremely strong and will not deflect under heavy loads.

I used melamine particleboard (PB) for my sheet material and hardwood trim to absorb the bumps and hits during heavy use. I decided to install adjustable plastic cabinet legs so I could level the fences.

This power miter saw station is perfect for my work. It has met all my needs and is a pleasure to use. I'm sure it will be a useful addition to your shop, as well.

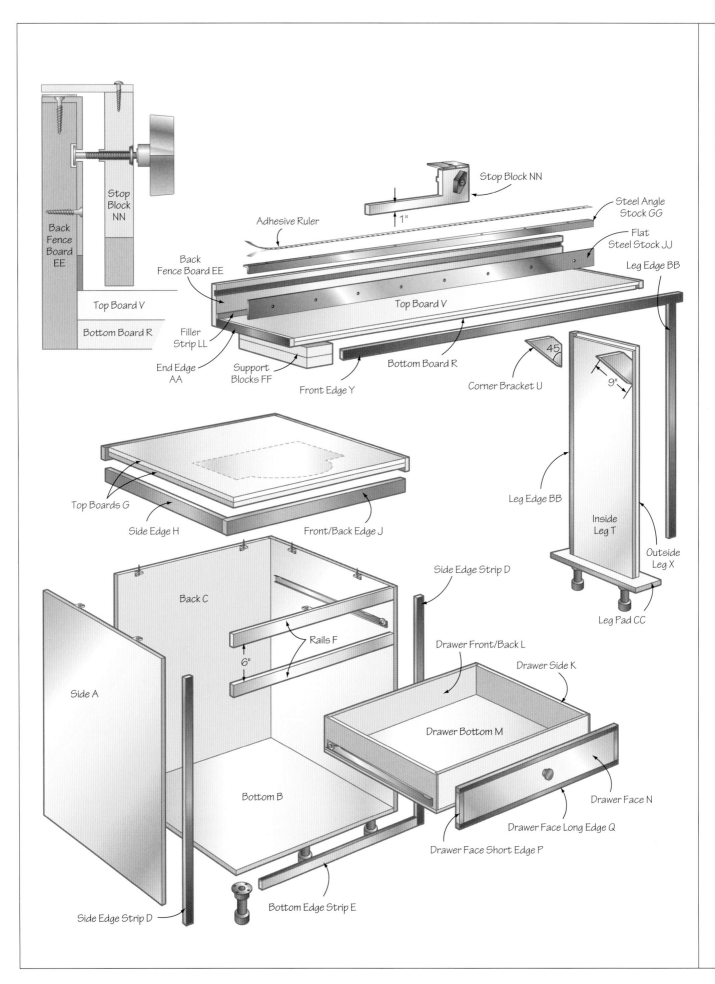

Stop Block NN

Back Fence Board EE

Stop Block NN

Top Board V

Bottom Board R

Adhesive Ruler

1"

Steel Angle Stock GG

Flat Steel Stock JJ

Leg Edge BB

Back Fence Board EE

Top Board V

Bottom Board R

Filler Strip LL

End Edge AA

Support Blocks FF

Front Edge Y

Corner Bracket U

45

9"

Leg Edge BB

Inside Leg T

Outside Leg X

Leg Pad CC

Top Boards G

Side Edge H

Front/Back Edge J

Back C

Rails F

6"

Side Edge Strip D

Drawer Front/Back L

Drawer Side K

Drawer Bottom M

Side A

Bottom B

Drawer Face N

Drawer Face Long Edge Q

Drawer Face Short Edge P

Side Edge Strip D

Bottom Edge Strip E

Schedule of Materials: Power Miter Saw Station

LTR.	NO.	ITEM	STOCK	INCHES T	(MM) T	INCHES W	(MM) W	INCHES L	(MM) L
Tower									
A	2	sides	melamine PB	⅝	16	24	610	36	914
B	1	bottom	melamine PB	⅝	16	26	660	24	610
C	1	back	melamine PB	⅝	16	26	660	35⅜	899
D	2	side edge strips	solid hardwood	¼	6	⅝	16	36	914
E	1	bottom edge strip	solid hardwood	¼	6	⅝	16	26	660
F	2	rails	solid hardwood	¼	6	1½	38	26	660
G	2	top boards	melamine PB	⅝	16	25¼	641	30½	775
H	2	side edges	solid hardwood	¼	6	1½	38	25¼	641
J	2	front & back edges	solid hardwood	¼	6	1½	38	32	813
K	2	drawer sides	melamine PB	⅝	16	4⅜	112	22	559
L	2	drawer front & back	melamine PB	⅝	16	4⅜	112	23¾	603
M	1	drawer bottom	melamine PB	⅝	16	22	559	25	635
N	1	drawer face	melamine PB	⅝	16	6½	165	26½	673
P	2	drawer face edges	solid hardwood	¼	6	⅝	16	6½	165
Q	2	drawer face edges	solid hardwood	¼	6	⅝	16	27	686
Fence Wings									
R	1	bottom board	melamine PB	⅝	16	7	178	71⅜	1813
S	1	bottom board	melamine PB	⅝	16	7	178	47⅜	1204
T	2	inside legs	melamine PB	⅝	16	7	178	38⅞	987
U	4	corner brackets	solid hardwood	¾	19	3½	89	9	229
V	1	top board	melamine PB	⅝	16	7	178	72	1829
W	1	top board	melamine PB	⅝	16	7	178	48	1219
X	2	outside legs	melamine PB	⅝	16	7	178	39½	1004
Y	1	front edge	solid hardwood	¾	19	1¼	31	73½	1867
Z	1	front edge	solid hardwood	¾	19	1¼	31	49½	1258
AA	4	end edges	solid hardwood	¾	19	1¼	31	7	178
BB	4	leg edges	solid hardwood	¾	19	1¼	31	38⅞	987
CC	2	leg pads	solid hardwood	¾	19	3½	89	8½	216
DD	1	back fence board	solid hardwood	¾	19	5¼	133	49½	1258
EE	1	back fence board	solid hardwood	¾	19	5¼	133	73½	1867
FF	2	support blocks	solid hardwood	1½	38	2¹¹⁄₁₆	69	6	152
GG	1	angle stock	steel	⅛	3	1×1	25x25	72	1829
HH	1	angle stock	steel	⅛	3	1×1	25x25	48	1219
JJ	1	flat stock	steel	⅛	3	2	51	72	1829
KK	1	flat stock	steel	⅛	3	2	51	48	1219
LL	1	filler strip	solid hardwood	⅛	3	¾	19	72	1829
MM	1	filler strip	solid hardwood	⅛	3	¾	19	48	1219
NN	2	stop blocks	solid hardwood	¾	19	3⅞	98	14	356

Supplies - inches

10 Adjustable plastic cabinet legs
1   22" Drawer glide set
7   Metal right-angle brackets
2   Metal self-sticking measuring tapes
1   $\frac{5}{16}$"-Diameter closet bolt set
2   Stop-block handles
1   Drawer handle
2   2" x 3" Plastic or Plexiglass
Metal washers
White iron-on edge tape
Screw cover caps
Screws as detailed
Glue
Wood plugs
2" PB screws
Biscuits or confirmat screws
$\frac{5}{8}$" Screws
Brad nails
Wood putty
1" Screws
3" Screws
Pan head screws and washers

Supplies - metric

10 Adjustable plastic cabinet legs
1   559mm Drawer glide set
7   Metal right-angle brackets
2   Metal self-sticking measuring tapes
1   8mm-Diameter closet bolt set
2   Stop-block handles
1   Drawer handle
2   51mm x 76mm Plastic or Plexiglass
Metal washers
White iron-on edge tape
Screw cover caps
Screws as detailed
Glue
Wood plugs
51mm PB screws
Biscuits or confirmat screws
16mm Screws
Brad nails
Wood putty
25mm Screws
76mm Screws
Pan head screws and washers

STEP 1 Cut the two sides A and bottom board B as detailed in the materials list. The joinery can be PB screws (on the right in the photo), biscuits (center) or confirmat screws (left). The confirmat screws are European-designed fasteners that are used to assemble melamine PB cabinetry. They are high-quality fasteners, but they do require a special step drill and accurate placement. The drill bits are expensive and brittle. The PB screws are designed to join this material, and the heads can be hidden with plastic cover caps.

I am using 2" PB screws placed 6" apart along the joint. Small white caps or white adhesive covers are available at woodworking and home stores.

SHOP tip

You can avoid splitting panels by keeping screws 1" away from any board end when joining sheet goods. Always drill a pilot hole for the screws to ensure maximum hold.

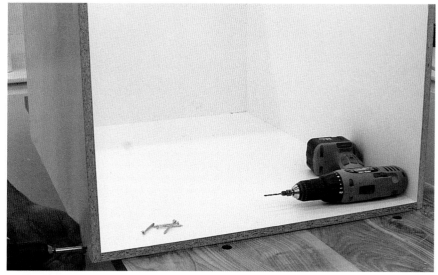

STEP 2 The inset backboard C is joined to the sides and bottom board with 2" PB screws. The back face of the backboard is flush with the back edges of the side and bottom boards.

STEP 3 I'm installing six adjustable plastic legs on my tower cabinet. The front legs are set back 3" and secured with four ⅝" screws. Position the flanges of the front and rear outside legs under the edges of the side boards. The load will be transferred directly to the sides, through the legs and onto the floor.

You can build and install a 4"-high base frame made with solid lumber or sheet material if there isn't a danger of liquid spills or water leaks on your shop floor. If water is an issue, or your shop floor isn't level, adjustable cabinet legs are the perfect solution.

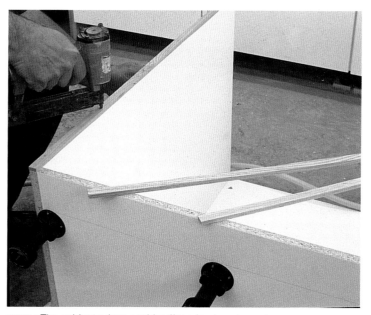

STEP 4 The cabinet edges could suffer a few knocks and bumps, so I installed hardwood edge strips D and E on the bottom and two side panels. Use glue and brad nails to secure the strips of wood. Fill the nail holes with wood putty and sand the strips smooth.

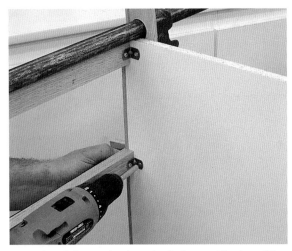

STEP 5 Install the two hardwood rails F, one at the top of the cabinet and the other below it, leaving a 6" space between the rails for a drawer. Secure the rails with right-angle brackets and ⅝" screws, or use pocket holes if you have a jig. Apply a little glue on the front edges to secure the rails to the side wood strips. Clamp until the adhesive cures.

STEP 6 Install seven right-angle brackets using ⅝" screws. One is located in the middle of the top rail and two on each of the back and side boards. These brackets will be used to secure the cabinet top.

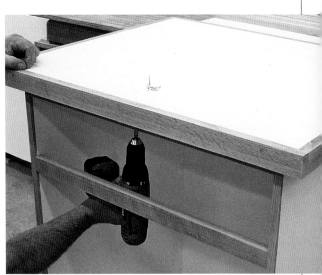

STEP 7 The cabinet top G is 32" wide by 26¾" deep overall. It is made with two layers of ⅝"-thick melamine PB, and joined with 1" screws from the underside. A ¾"-thick by 1½"-wide hardwood band, H and J, is applied to all four edges. Use glue and 2" screws in a ⅜" counterbored hole and fill the holes with wood plugs. You can also use biscuits (plate joinery) if you prefer that method.

STEP 8 Attach the banded top to the cabinet using 1" screws through the right-angle brackets previously installed. The top overhangs the back by ¾" and by 2⅜" on each side.

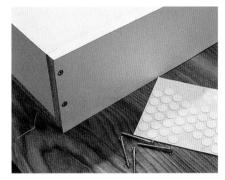

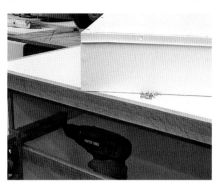

STEP 9 Drawer boxes are commonly 1" less in height and width when using most ¾-extension drawer glide sets. This rule is also applied to most full-extension drawer glide sets. However, read the installation instructions with your hardware before cutting the drawer box parts.

Cut the drawer box parts K through M and apply iron-on edge tape to the upper edges of the side, back and front boards. The side edges of the bottom board also require edge tape.

STEP 10 Join the sides to the back and front boards using 2" PB screws. The bottom board is also installed using 2" screws about 8" apart. Cut the bottom board square and it will ensure that your drawer box is square. The box should be 5" high by 25" wide by 22" deep. The screw heads can be covered with plastic caps or white stick-on covers. Refer to chapter one for more details.

STEP 11 Mount the drawer glide runners on the cabinet sides, attach the two drawer runners to the box using ⅝" screws and test fit your drawer. The cabinet runners can be installed using a straight line made with a carpenter's square, or a drawer glide-mounting jig.

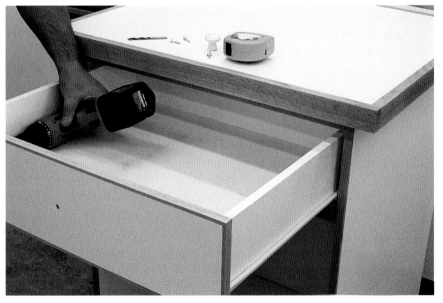

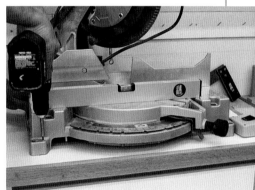

STEP 13 Place the tower section where it will be used in your shop and level the cabinet front to back and side to side. Center the miter saw on the top and secure it with screws or bolts. It's difficult to generalize on methods to secure your saw because so many models are available. However, once you have it installed trace an outline on the top with a permanent marker. If the saw has to be removed from the station, it can easily be returned to the same position using the trace lines.

STEP 12 The finished size of the drawer face is 7" high by 27" wide. I made my drawer face with ⅝"-thick melamine PB and ¼"-thick by ⅝"-wide hardwood strips on all four edges. The strips were installed with glue and brad nails. To ensure perfect drawer-face alignment, drill the handle or knob holes in the drawer face only. Put the drawer box in the cabinet, hold the drawer face in its correct position, and drive screws through the holes securing it to the drawer box. Then carefully open the drawer and secure the face by driving 1" screws through the drawer box front board into the back of the drawer face. Remove the screw (or screws) in the handle holes and drill through the drawer box. Finally, install the handle to complete the installation.

STEP 14 The right-side fence platform on my station will be 6' long, and the left side will be 4' long. Both will be built with 7"-wide melamine PB and edged with ¾" hardwood that's 1¼" wide so it will cover the double-thickness melamine PB pieces. The lengths of these fence platforms are determined by the amount of space you have available and the type of cutting you do in your shop. Change the lengths of the horizontal boards to suit your shop.

Cut the inside legs T and bottom boards R and S to size. Attach the horizontal bottom shelves to the inside leg top ends using 2" PB screws. Cut the four brackets U and attach two at each corner using 2" screws.

STEP 15 Cut the two top boards V and W, as well as the two outside legs X, to size. Attach the boards as shown in the drawing, using 1" screws from the underside of the bottom top board and back side of the inside leg board. The photo shows proper placement of the boards with the fence assembly's top board resting upside down on the workbench. Two screws, 8" apart and placed in 1" from the edges, will create a solid melamine "sandwich." Hide the screw heads on the legs with plastic caps or stickers.

STEP 16 All the exposed edges, with the exception of the two back edges on the horizontal platforms, are banded with ¾"-thick by 1¼"-wide hardwood. Use glue and screws, in counterbored holes, to attach the hardwood to the front and ends of both platforms, as well as the back and front edges of the legs. Fill the screw head holes with wood plugs.

STEP 17 The size of the leg pad CC will depend on the style of leg you install. My legs require a wide base so I attached a 3½"-wide pad with screws and glue. The legs are secured with four ⅝" screws.

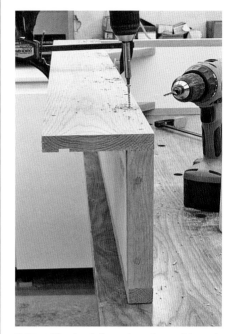

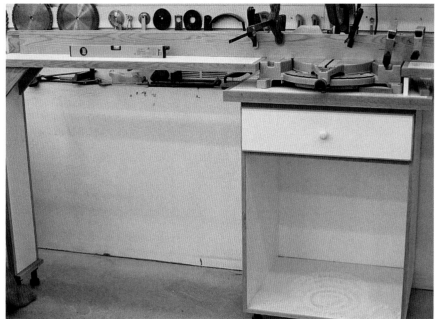

STEP 18 The back fence boards must be cut and grooved before being attached. The groove is ½" wide by ⅛" deep and is located ¾" down from the top edge of each fence board. Attach the fence boards DD and EE with glue and 2" screws. The boards are installed with the groove at the top and facing inward toward the platform. The bottom of each fence board is flush with the bottom face of the lower melamine fence platform boards R and S.

STEP 19 Clamp a long straightedge across the saw bed. Level each fence platform by blocking the end that rests on the tower tabletop and adjusting the legs at the ends. The fence platforms must be flush with the saw platform. Set the face of the platform fences ⅛" behind the saw fence because we will be installing ⅛"-thick steel on the fence.

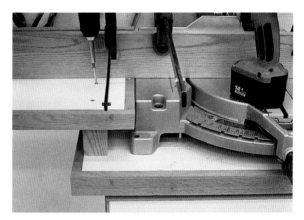

STEP 20 Cut two support blocks FF (the block thickness I needed to match my saw's platform was 2¹¹⁄₁₆") and attach them to the tower tabletop with screws driven from the underside of that top. Use 3" screws to secure the platforms to each block, making certain the fence platforms are level with the saw's platform.

STEP 21 The next step is to build a stop-block system. First, drill and attach ⅛"-thick steel angle stock parts GG and HH on the top of each platform fence board. Steel angle and flat stock is available at most hardware and home stores. The steel angle stock is ⅞" wide on the inside face and will rest ⅛" lower than the top of the fence groove. Be sure to countersink the screw heads so the adhesive steel ruler will lay flat on top of the angle stock.

SHOP tip

Construct or buy a wall bracket if you are concerned about bumping the platforms with heavy lumber. The platforms are solid and stable, but you may want extra support, so attach a bracket between the legs and a wall. The miter station tower can also be anchored to the wall for extra stability, however, the tower and fence platforms are rigid and will remain aligned under normal usage.

STEP 22 Drill and countersink the ⅛"-thick by 2"-wide steel flat stock pieces JJ and KK. The holes should be about 6" apart and countersunk so the screw heads are below the stock's surface. Attach the flat steel to the back fence boards using ⅝" screws.

The bolts that will be used for the stop assemblies are a toilet or closet bolt set; they are ⁵⁄₁₆"-diameter bolts with large, flat oval heads. Clamp the flat steel below the angle stock with a bolt in the groove. The bolts should move freely, but you shouldn't be able to pull them out.

STEP 23 Once the steel pieces have been installed and the bolts are moving freely along the length of each track, cut and install filler strips LL and MM. These strips will make the fence flush from top to bottom. Use glue and brad nails to secure the strips.

STEP 24 Install self-sticking measuring tapes on top of each angle iron. You'll need left-to-right and right-to-left reading tapes. The zero mark on each ruler should align with the end of each angle iron closest to the miter saw.

STEP 25 Cut stop-block boards NN as shown in the materials list. They will be trimmed to size on the miter station. Set the table saw fence for a ⅝"-thick cut with the blade 1" high. Run both boards through the saw, on edge. Reset the blade 2½" high and run both boards through the saw once again after flipping them. The result will be a ⅛"-thick by ¼"-wide tenon on the back face of each board. The tenon will slide in the space between both pieces of steel and stabilize the stop block.

SHOP tip

You can use aluminum stock, but steel is about one-half the cost and is much stronger. The same fence system can also be built using an aluminum T-track set into a groove in the back fence board. I've opted for steel in this case because it strengthens the fence platforms.

STEP 26 Cut the stop-block boards on a band saw or with a jigsaw, as shown. The first 3" of the board should be full height and the remainder 1" high. Remember that you'll need a right and left stop-block assembly, so pay close attention to how the cut lines are laid out on each board.

STEP 27 Drill a ⅜"-diameter hole through the middle of each tenon on both stop blocks. The holes should be centered on the width of the full-height portion of each block. Use a closet bolt and washer with a suitable knob to attach each block. I found the knobs at my local hardware store with a thread pattern that matched the closet bolt set. Most woodworking stores also carry these knobs in many styles.

STEP 28 The stop-block position is determined by a clear plastic indicator screwed to the top of each stop block. Clear plastic or Plexiglass is available at craft and plastic supply stores.

Cut two pieces each 2" wide by 3" long. Scribe a fine line in the plastic with an awl or other sharp tool. Use a permanent marker to fill the scratch with ink. Attach the indicator to the stop block with pan head screws and washers in oval-shaped holes that will allow side-to-side adjustment. Align the mark on the plastic indicator to zero on the tape measure and trim the tongue on the stop block with your miter saw. That's your zero measurement for each block, and if you need to fine-tune the adjustment, loosen the screws and move the plastic indicator.

CONSTRUCTION notes

I decided to use steel for these long fence platforms because I didn't want any deflection, and the result was impressive. Both fence systems are stable and rigid.

The fence platforms are high enough so I can store other workstations underneath, which is a real bonus in any shop. I used melamine PB for the field and oak hardwood for the edges; however, any sheet material and wood banding can be used. The smooth surface of the melamine makes it easy to slide the boards being cut, but materials such as medium-density fiberboard will serve the same purpose.

The dimensions of the tower can be changed if you find the height unsuitable. My tower interior width was designed to hold a large plastic pail for scraps, but it can be narrower if you don't need a scrap pail. My platform is wide because my 12" miter saw has a large bed. Smaller saws are common, so design your tower top to hold the saw you own. I don't think there are much wider miter saws on the market, but it's well worth taking the time to measure your saw before building the tower.

You can include many other features in your design. For example, a rack could be attached to the outside face of the side boards to hold saw blades. Or the drawer could be divided with partitions for various tools and documents that are needed for your saw. I also considered adding another cabinet beside the tower with adjustable shelves for storing small cutoffs that can be used for other projects.

If you don't have access to adjustable legs, or prefer a solid base, you can construct one with 2x4 material or plywood. The steel, closet bolts and knobs are common hardware items and should be readily available at your local hardware store.

Multifunction Power Tool Cabinet

A power tool stand is a great addition to any workshop; however, if you have limited space, need to move the tools out of the way for your car or don't use certain tools on a regular basis, a dedicated power tool station is not much use. I think you'll find this tool cabinet answers all those needs.

This versatile tool cabinet has a removable platform that locks securely into place in less than a minute. It can be used with dozens of power tools that are secured to individual mounting boards. The cabinet has four locking wheels, an open shelf for accessories, and a drawer to store all the documentation and extra parts that come with your tools.

The cabinet is built with tough, inexpensive 5⁄8" melamine particleboard (PB) and hardwood edging so it will last for years. It can be tucked away in a corner or stored under the miter saw station wings described in chapter three.

The top and tool platforms are constructed using ¾"-thick medium-density fiberboard (MDF), which is another inexpensive sheet material. The drawer is 5⁄8" melamine PB and mounted on ¾-extension, bottom-mount drawer glides. The cabinet also has enough room to store a second power tool on its mounting platform, in the bottom section.

This has been one of the most valuable cabinets I've built for my shop. Moving the power tools to my work area, with all the accessories on board where I can quickly locate them, is a real benefit, and I'm enjoying my work even more. I was so pleased with this mobile tool cabinet that I built two and may build another in the near future. I hope you'll find it just as useful and build one or two for your shop.

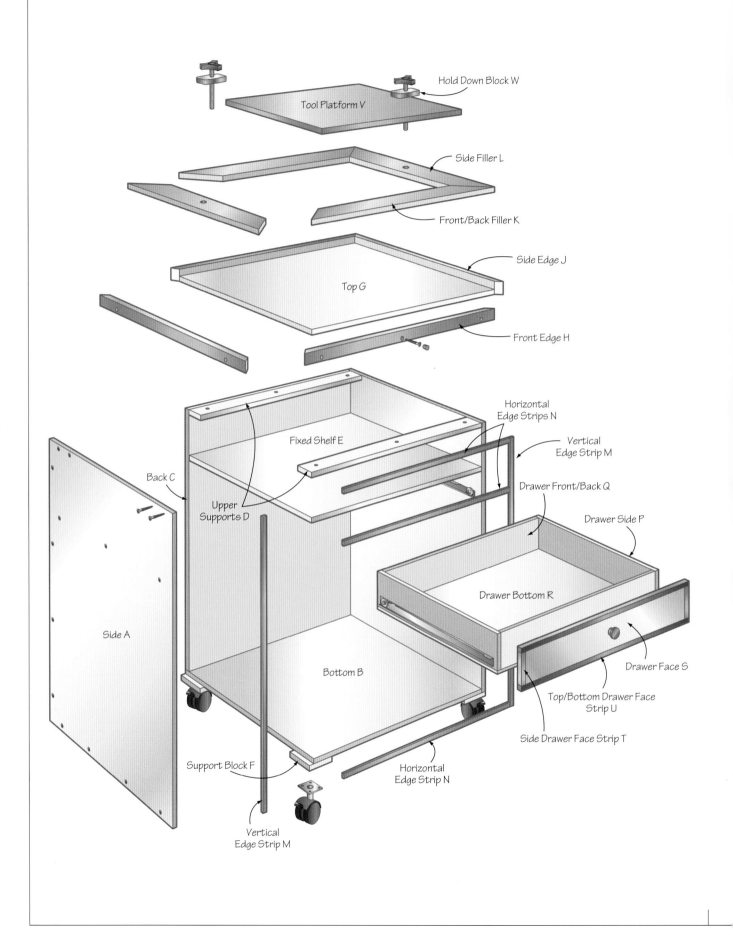

Hold Down Block W

Tool Platform V

Side Filler L

Front/Back Filler K

Side Edge J

Top G

Front Edge H

Horizontal Edge Strips N

Vertical Edge Strip M

Fixed Shelf E

Drawer Front/Back Q

Back C

Drawer Side P

Upper Supports D

Side A

Drawer Bottom R

Bottom B

Drawer Face S

Top/Bottom Drawer Face Strip U

Side Drawer Face Strip T

Support Block F

Horizontal Edge Strip N

Vertical Edge Strip M

Schedule of Materials: Multifunction Power Tool Cabinet

LTR.	NO.	ITEM	STOCK	INCHES T	(MM) T	INCHES W	(MM) W	INCHES L	(MM) L	
A	2	sides	melamine PB	5/8	16	20	508	32	813	
B	1	bottom	melamine PB	5/8	16	20	508	26	660	
C	1	back	melamine PB	5/8	16	26	660	31 3/8	797	
D	2	upper supports	melamine PB	5/8	16	4	102	26	660	
E	1	fixed shelf	melamine PB	5/8	16	19 3/8	493	26	660	
F	4	support blocks	hardwood	3/4	19	3 1/2	89	3 1/2	89	
G	1	top	melamine PB	5/8	16	21	533	30	762	
H	2	front & back top edges	hardwood	3/4	19	1 3/8	35	31 1/2	800	angle-cut
J	2	side edges	hardwood	3/4	19	1 3/8	35	22 1/2	572	angle-cut
K	2	front & back top fillers	MDF	3/4	19	2 1/4	57	30	762	angle-cut
L	2	side fillers	MDF	3/4	19	2 1/4	57	21	533	angle-cut
M	2	vertical edge strips	hardwood	1/4	6	5/8	16	32	813	
N	3	horizontal edge strips	hardwood	1/4	6	5/8	16	26	660	
P	2	drawer sides	melamine PB	5/8	16	4 3/8	112	18	457	
Q	2	drawer front & back	melamine PB	5/8	16	4 3/8	112	23 3/4	603	
R	1	drawer bottom	melamine PB	5/8	16	18	457	25	635	
S	1	drawer face	melamine PB	5/8	16	6 1/2	165	26 1/2	673	
T	2	side drawer face strips	hardwood	1/4	6	5/8	16	6 1/2	165	
U	2	top/bott drwr face strips	hardwood	1/4	6	5/8	16	27	686	
V	3	tool platforms	MDF	3/4	19	16 1/2	419	25 1/2	648	
W	2	hold-down blocks	hardwood	3/4	19	1 1/2	38	3	76	

Supplies - inches

4 Locking wheel casters

1 – 18" Drawer glide set

2 Knobs, 1/4"-diameter thread

2 Hanger bolts, 2 1/2"-long x 1/4"-diameter thread

2 – 1/4" Metal washers

White iron-on edge tape

Screw cover caps

Screws as detailed

Glue

Wood plugs

2" Screws

Biscuits

Dowels

1 1/4" Screws

1" Screws

Brad nails

Wood putty

5/8" Screws

Supplies - metric

4 Locking wheel casters

1 – 457mm Drawer glide set

2 Knobs, 6mm-diameter thread

2 Hanger bolts, 64mm-long x 6mm-diameter thread

2 – 6mm Metal washers

White iron-on edge tape

Screw cover caps

Screws as detailed

Glue

Wood plugs

51mm Screws

Biscuits

Dowels

32mm Screws

25mm Screws

Brad nails

Wood putty

16mm Screws

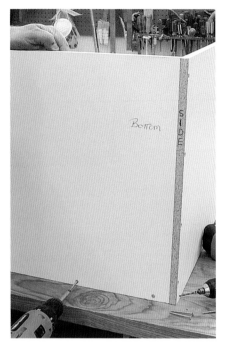

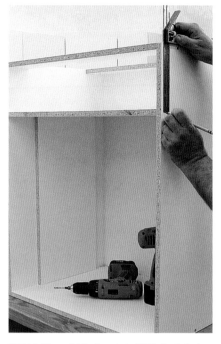

STEP 1 Cut the sides A, bottom B and back C to the sizes listed in the materials list using ⅝" melamine PB. Attach the sides to the bottom board using 2" PB screws in pilot holes spaced 6" apart. The inset backboard is also attached with screws through the side and bottom boards.

The joinery can be done with PB screws, biscuits or dowels and glue. The screw heads can be covered with plastic or self-adhesive cover caps.

STEP 2 The two upper supports D are added so the cabinet sides remain parallel at the top. They will also be used to secure the top board. Cut the two supports to length, installing the front board flush with the edges of the side panels. Secure the boards with 2" PB screws, placed 1" in from each edge to avoid splitting the boards. Drill through-holes for the screws, which will be used to secure the top.

STEP 3 The middle fixed shelf E is installed 6" below the bottom surface of the upper supports. Holding a shelf accurately in place is difficult, so I've cut two 24⅛"-high temporary spacers to properly locate the shelf. Use a square to mark the screw position in the center of the fixed shelf's edge on the side and back panels. Drive 2" screws, in pilot holes, through the panels to secure the shelf. Cover the screw heads with caps.

SHOP tip

Many woodworkers have a sliding table for crosscutting panels; however, it isn't safe to use the fence and another guide device when crosscutting because there's a possibility that the board will bind in the blade and be thrown backwards. Instead you can use the measuring feature on your saw fence by adding a stop block. The panel being cut on a sliding table will leave the block before it completes the cut, making the operation safe. Remember to add 1" (with a 1"-thick block) to the fence distance to account for the stop-block thickness.

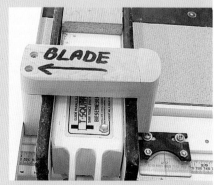

STEP 4 Attach four caster support blocks F on the corners of the cabinet. Position the blocks so the outside edges are flush with the outside edges of the cabinet. Use 2" screws on the outside edges through the blocks and into the back or side boards. The inner edges are secured with 1¼" screws into the bottom board.

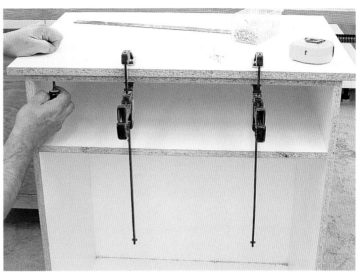

STEP 5 Mount four locking casters on the blocks using 1¼" screws or lag bolts.

STEP 6 Attach the cabinet top G with an overhang of ½" on the front and back. The sides will have an overhang of 1⅜". Use 1" screws through the upper supports D to secure the top board.

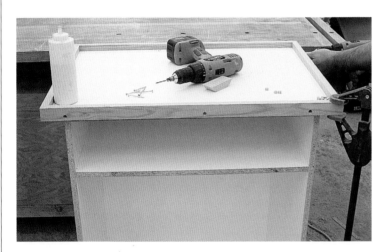

STEP 7 The top board G is banded with ¾"-thick by 1⅜"-high hardwood. The hardwood edge is flush with the bottom face of the top board and ¾" above the top's surface. Cut the corners of the hardwood banding at 45° and secure them with biscuits and glue or, as I'm using, screws and glue. Fill the counterbored holes with wood plugs and sand smooth.

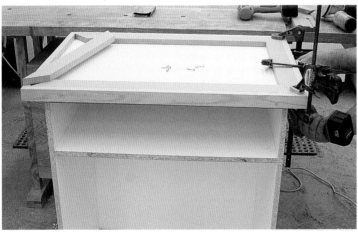

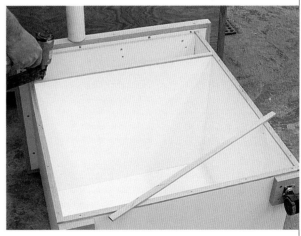

STEP 8 The tabletop fillers K and L are ¾" MDF. One sheet of 4x8 MDF has enough material for six tool platforms as well as the 2¼"-wide filler boards. The corners are joined at 45°, and the fillers are held in place with 1¼" screws from the underside of the tabletop.

STEP 9 Lay the cabinet on its back and trim the edges with ¼"-thick by ⅝"-wide hardwood strips M and N. Attach the strips with glue and brad nails. Fill the nail holes with wood putty and sand smooth.

STEP 10 The next step is to build an accessory drawer under the fixed shelf. The drawer box is 5" high by 18" deep and 1" narrower than the inside cabinet width, or 25". It will be installed with bottom-mounted ¾-extension drawer glides. The drawer box is constructed using ⅝"-thick melamine PB.

Cut the drawer sides P, front and back Q and drawer bottom R. Use iron-on edge tape to cover the top edges of the sides, back and front boards, as well as the side edges of the bottom board.

STEP 11 Attach the drawer box sides to the back and front boards using 2" PB screws in pilot holes. Attach the bottom using 2" PB screws.

STEP 13 The drawer face S is 2" wider and 2" higher than the drawer box, or 27" wide by 7" high. The drawer face is trimmed with ¼"-thick by ⅝"-wide hardwood strips. To arrive at the final height, cut the melamine PB center ½" less in width and height.

Attach the edge strips T and U with glue and brad nails. Fill the holes with wood putty and sand the edges smooth.

STEP 12 Install the drawer glide hardware following the manufacturer's instructions. The cabinet runners are installed with the bottom track 6" below the fixed storage shelf E. Use a carpenter's square to draw a screw-hole reference line or a drawer glide-mounting jig to install the runners with ⅝" screws.

STEP 14 Attach the face to the drawer box using 1" screws through the back side of the drawer box front board. I drill the handle hole (or holes) in my drawer face and drive a screw through that hole to temporarily secure the face board in the proper position. Then I gently open the drawer and install the 1" screws through the back. Once the face is secure, I remove the screw from the handle hole and drill completely through the drawer box to install a knob or handle.

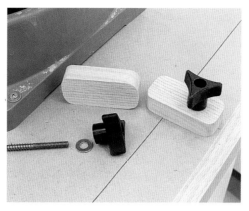

CONSTRUCTION
notes

Most of the benchtop power tools in my shop will fit on the 16½"-deep by 25½"-wide platforms; however, the cabinet size should meet your needs. Build it to the dimensions shown in this chapter or change the width, height or depth as needed. If you do alter the platform size, be sure it will fit in the lower section of the cabinet to take advantage of all the storage space.

I used melamine particleboard and medium-density fiberboard, but any sheet material you feel comfortable with will work just as well. I like these materials because they are inexpensive and, in the case of melamine PB, already finished with a tough coating. Both materials can be securely joined using PB screws.

These power tool stations are mobile but can be made stationary by replacing the wheels with a fixed base. They'll work just as well against a wall if you have the space available. I opted for mobile units because they can be tucked away under the wings of my power miter saw station, built in chapter three.

STEP 16 The tool platforms V are ¾"-thick MDF. I cut three platforms for each of my two mobile tool stations. However, you can make as many as you need to mount your power tools. A platform without a tool can be used as a mobile worktable when needed.

STEP 16 The tool platforms are held in place with a simple lock assembly. Screw a 2½"-long by ¼"-diameter hanger bolt into the side fillers, 1" back from the inside edge. Cut and round over the corners of a ¾"-thick by 3"-long piece of hardwood. Drill a 5⁄16"-diameter hole in this hold-down block W, 1" from an end, and slip it over the hanger bolt. Place a metal washer on the bolt and attach a ¼"-diameter threaded knob. One block on each side will secure the tool platform when the knobs are tightened.

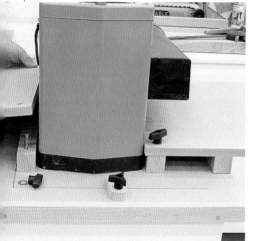

STEP 17 Benchtop power tools, like the planer shown in this photograph, require infeed and outfeed tables. If they were fixed in place, the tool would be larger than the platform's footprint, making storage difficult. You can easily build removable platforms using hanger bolts, spacer cleats and knobs. In this example my feed tables are longer than the factory-supplied models and will provide more support for the material being machined.

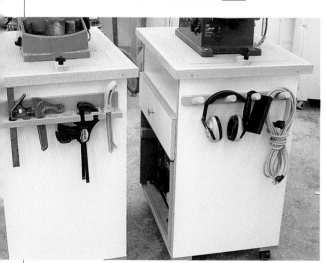

STEP 18 Dozens of different tool holders can be attached to the sides of your mobile power tool cabinets. Extension cords, safety equipment and other accessories required when working with different benchtop power tools can be installed.

Router Table Cabinet

I've seen a lot of router table systems, tried many and had a number of different designs in my shop over the years. However, I always found something lacking in the designs and often promised myself that I would build a router table cabinet to suit my needs one day. Well, that day has arrived, and I'm pleased with the results.

My list of design demands included an adjustable fence that had an opening range of at least 12". How many times have you wanted to run a groove in a wide board and couldn't because your router fence system opened only a couple of inches? My dream table had to have a miter slide track, be at least 35" high and have a large, solid-surface table to support boards properly. I was really tired of balancing large panels on small flimsy tables.

Accessory storage and proper dust collection rounded out my list of "wants" for the ideal router cabinet. I hesitate to say ultimate router station because there's always something missing that I'll discover later, but this cabinet is close to perfect for my work and it didn't cost a fortune to build.

I used ¾"-thick MDF sheet material. It's a great board for this application because the MDF is heavy, which will keep the cabinet stable, and it's easy to machine. I've detailed two leg options, one for a movable cabinet and the other for a cabinet that will be permanently located. The knobs and aluminum tracks are available at all woodworking outlets and are reasonably priced.

Have fun building of this router cabinet. You'll have easy access to the router and good dust collection. I'm sure you'll appreciate the bit storage slide-outs and great storage drawers for all your router accessories.

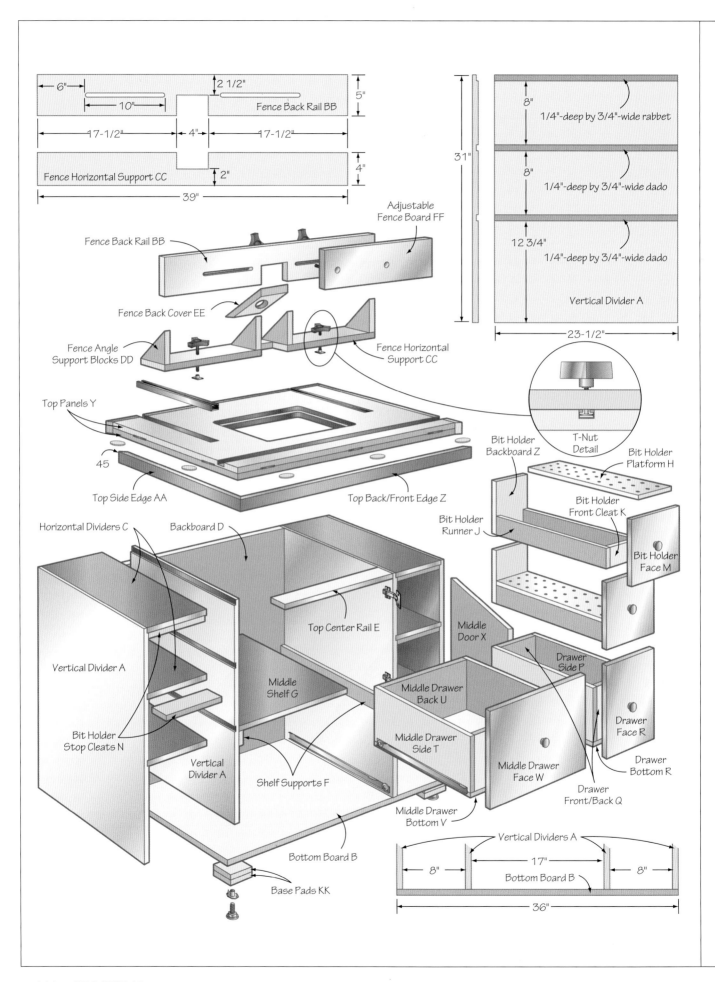

6"
10"
2 1/2"
5"
Fence Back Rail BB
17-1/2"
4"
17-1/2"
Fence Horizontal Support CC
2"
4"
39"

8"
1/4"-deep by 3/4"-wide rabbet
31"
8"
1/4"-deep by 3/4"-wide dado
12 3/4"
1/4"-deep by 3/4"-wide dado
Vertical Divider A
23-1/2"

Fence Back Rail BB
Adjustable Fence Board FF
Fence Back Cover EE
Fence Angle Support Blocks DD
Fence Horizontal Support CC

T-Nut Detail

Top Panels Y
45
Top Side Edge AA
Top Back/Front Edge Z

Bit Holder Backboard Z
Bit Holder Platform H
Bit Holder Front Cleat K
Bit Holder Runner J
Bit Holder Face M

Horizontal Dividers C
Backboard D
Top Center Rail E
Vertical Divider A
Middle Shelf G
Bit Holder Stop Cleats N
Vertical Divider A
Shelf Supports F
Middle Door X
Middle Drawer Back U
Drawer Side P
Middle Drawer Side T
Drawer Face R
Middle Drawer Face W
Drawer Bottom R
Drawer Front/Back Q
Middle Drawer Bottom V
Bottom Board B
Base Pads KK

Vertical Dividers A
8"
17"
8"
Bottom Board B
36"

Schedule of Materials: Router Table Cabinet

LTR.	NO.	ITEM	STOCK	INCHES T	(MM) T	INCHES W	(MM) W	INCHES L	(MM) L	COMMENTS
A	4	vertical dividers	MDF	¾	19	23½	597	31	787	
B	1	bottom board	MDF	¾	19	23½	597	36	914	
C	6	horizontal dividers	MDF	¾	19	8½	216	23½	597	
D	1	backboard	MDF	¾	19	31¾	806	36	914	
E	1	top center rail	MDF	¾	19	3	76	17	432	
F	2	shelf supports	MDF	¾	19	3	76	23½	597	
G	1	middle shelf	MDF	¾	19	17	432	23½	597	
H	4	bit holder platforms	MDF	¾	19	7¹⁵/₁₆	202	22	559	
J	8	bit holder runners	MDF	¾	19	2½	64	22	559	
K	4	bit holder front cleats	MDF	¾	19	2½	64	6⁷/₁₆	163	
L	4	bit holder backboards	MDF	¾	19	7¹⁵/₁₆	202	7¹⁵/₁₆	202	
M	4	bit holder front faces	MDF	¾	19	9	229	8½	216	
N	4	bit holder stop cleats	MDF	¾	19	2	51	8	203	
P	4	drawer sides	MDF	¾	19	9¼	235	22	559	
Q	4	drawer fronts & backs	MDF	¾	19	9¼	235	5½	140	
R	2	drawer bottoms	MDF	¾	19	7	178	22	559	
S	2	drawer faces	MDF	¾	19	9	229	13⅞	352	
T	2	middle drawer sides	MDF	¾	19	7¾	197	22	559	
U	2	drawer front & back	MDF	¾	19	7¾	197	14½	369	
V	1	drawer bottom	MDF	¾	19	16	406	22	559	
W	1	middle drawer face	MDF	¾	19	17¾	451	13⅞	352	
X	1	middle door	MDF	¾	19	17¾	451	17¼	438	
Y	2	top panels	MDF	¾	19	37¾	959	27¾	705	
Z	2	top back & front edges	hardwood	¾	19	1½	38	39¼	997	
AA	2	top side edges	hardwood	¾	19	1½	38	29¼	743	
BB	1	fence back rail	MDF	¾	19	5	127	39	991	
CC	1	fence horizontal support	MDF	¾	19	4	102	39	991	
DD	4	fence angle support blocks	MDF	¾	19	4	102	4	102	angle-cut
EE	1	fence back cover	MDF	¾	19	4	102	5¼	133	angle-cut
FF	2	adjustable fence boards	MDF	¾	19	5	127	19½	496	
		Base Option #1								
GG	2	sides	MDF	¾	19	3	76	20	508	
HH	2	front & back boards	MDF	¾	19	3	76	4½	115	
JJ	1	top	MDF	¾	19	6	152	20	508	
	2	heavy-duty wheels, 3¾" high								
		Base Option #2								
KK	8	base pads	MDF	¾	19	3	76	3	76	
	4	metal adjustable leveling feet								

Supplies - inches

- 4 Drawer knobs or pulls
- 3 Sets of 22" drawer glides
- 2 107° Hidden hinges and plates
- 1 48" -Long aluminum miter slide track
- 1 48" -Long aluminum T-track
- 6 1" by ¼" -Diameter threaded knobs
- 1 Power bar with switch

1½" PB screws as detailed

⅝" PB screws as detailed

Glue

Pocket screws

Brad nails

2" Screws

T-nuts

Supplies - metric

- 4 Drawer knobs or pulls
- 3 Sets of 559mm drawer glides
- 2 107° Hidden hinges and plates
- 1 1219mm-Long aluminum miter slide track
- 1 1219mm-Long aluminum T-track
- 6 25mm by 6mm-Diameter threaded knobs
- 1 Power bar with switch

38mm PB screws as detailed

16mm PB screws as detailed

Glue

Pocket screws

Brad nails

51mm Screws

T-nuts

STEP 1 Prepare the four vertical dividers A by cutting them to size and forming the dadoes and rabbets in each panel as shown. All the rabbets and dadoes are ¾" wide by ¼" deep.

STEP 2 The bottom board B is secured to the dividers with glue and 1½" screws in pilot holes. Align the two sets of dividers, spaced 8" apart, with the dadoes and rabbets facing each other. The middle section should be 17" wide between panels. Keep the screws 1" away from any panel end and use four screws per divider, driven through the bottom board.

STEP 3 Install the six horizontal dividers C in the dadoes and rabbets. Use glue and clamps to secure the sections.

STEP 4 Attach the backboard D to the cabinet using glue and 1½" screws. If you've carefully cut the back panel square, the cabinet will be properly aligned.

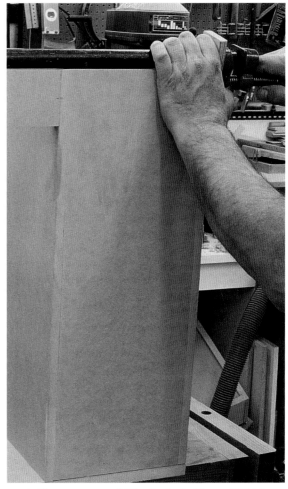

STEP 5 The top center rail E is attached with one ¾"-thick edge facing forward. Secure it with biscuits, or pocket screws and glue if you don't have a biscuit joiner. This rail will be attached to the underside of the tabletop.

This cabinet is on its back with the top facing the camera.

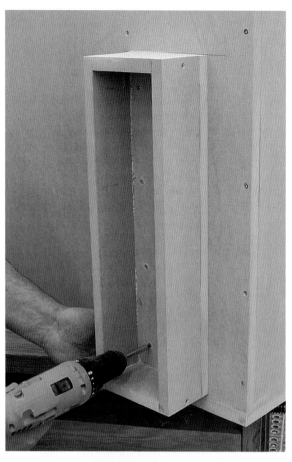

STEP 7 The other half of base option #1 is a box made with ¾" MDF using the parts GG, HH and JJ. It's attached to the bottom of the cabinet with 1¼" screws and glue. If the cabinet has to be moved often, you can lift the fixed base end and push it along the floor on the wheels.

The height of my fixed base portion is 3¾" to match the wheel height. If you do use this setup, purchase the wheels first so the correct height can be verified. After installing both options, I've decided to use base #2 on my cabinet, as described in step 29.

STEP 6 If you plan to use base option #1, attach two heavy-duty locking wheel assemblies to one side of the cabinet.

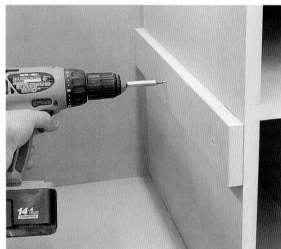

STEP 8 Install the two shelf supports F in the middle section. They are secured with glue and 1¼" screws. Their top edges are 12¾" above the bottom board. Cut the middle shelf G to the size indicated in the materials list and secure it to the cleats with glue and brad nails.

STEP 9 The four bit holder slide-outs are made with ¾"-thick MDF. Each holder board has a series of holes for ¼"- and ½"-diameter router bits. I spaced my holes 2" apart with the two outside rows 1½" in from each board's edge and the third row in the center.

The holder platforms H are attached to the runners J with glue and 1½" screws. The runners are flush with the outside long edges of the holder platforms. A front lower cleat K is also attached to the holder platform in the same way. The backboards L are attached to the rear of each assembly with glue and 1½" screws. Use a ¼" roundover bit in your router to soften the front edges of the slide-out faces M. Once the face is aligned on the slide-out, attach each face with 1¼" screws through the front lower cleat.

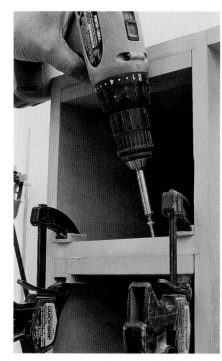

STEP 10 Cut and attach the four stop cleats N with glue and 1¼"-long screws. These cleats will stop the slide-out when fully extended. When it's necessary to remove or install the slide-outs, simply tip them upward to move past the stop cleats.

STEP 11 The two outside lower drawer boxes are 7" wide by 10" high by 22" deep and made with ¾"-thick MDF. Attach the drawer sides P to the back and front boards Q using glue and 1½" screws. The bottom boards R are also secured to the sides, front and bottom board edges with 1½" screws and glue to form the drawer boxes. Use 22" bottom-mount drawer glides, or full-extension glides if you prefer, to install the drawer boxes in the cabinet.

STEP 12 The lower outside drawer box faces S have their front edges rounded over using a ¼" router bit. They are secured to the drawer boxes with 1¼" screws through the inside of the box. Install the faces so they are aligned with the slide-out fronts, leaving a ⅛" gap between each front.

STEP 13 The lower middle drawer box is 8½" high by 16" wide by 22" deep. Build the box using ¾" MDF with parts T, U and V following the same steps as the outside lower drawer boxes. Mount this box using 22" drawer glides.

STEP 14 Round over the front edges of drawer face W using a ¼" router bit. Attach it to the drawer box with 1¼" screws, being careful to leave equal spacing on both sides, with its top aligned to the two outside drawer faces.

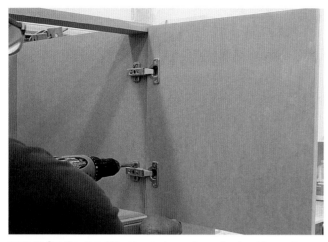

STEP 15 Cut the door X to size and round over the front face edges. I used full-overlay 107° hinges with standard mounting plates. Drill 35mm holes, ⅛" from the door edge, to secure the hinges. Hold the door in its normally open position, with a ⅛"-thick spacer between the door and cabinet edge, and secure the mounting plates with ⅝" screws.

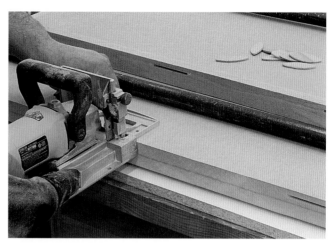

STEP 16 The top is made by gluing two ¾"-thick MDF panels together. Cut both panels Y a little oversize so they can be trimmed to a finished size when the adhesive has cured. The top is banded with 1½"-high by ¾"-thick hardwood and is secured in place with biscuits. Cut the edges Z and AA to size with 45° miters on each end to join the corners.

STEP 17 Turn the top upside down on the router cabinet. It should overhang the front edge by 1½" and the sides by 1⅝". I will be using a Rout-R-Lift plate made by JessEm Tool Company, but any plate can be installed using the following method. Place the router plate on the center of the table and 5" back from the front edge of the top. Fasten strips of wood around the plate with screws. These strips will be used as a template to guide your router.

STEP 18 The router base should have a bushing guide installed to run against the strips of wood. The size of the bushing should equal the depth of cut for the wing or slot cutter bit that will be used to form a groove on the top side of the table to inset the router plate flush with the top face. My wing bit cuts ½" deep, so I want the hole to be smaller than the strip edges by ½" on all sides. Cut the hole using the guide bushing and router bit.

STEP 19 Flip the top right side up and use the wing cutter to groove the top. The router plate should be flush with the tabletop's surface. I hand-formed the corners to match my router plate. It may also be necessary in your case to use a sharp knife and chisel to carve the corners. Fasten the top to the cabinet using 2" screws through the horizontal supports and middle top rail.

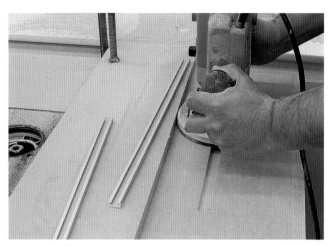

STEP 20 I installed a ¾" miter slide track in my tabletop. Cut the groove for the slide track as close to the front edge of your router plate as possible. This track required a 1"-wide groove cut parallel to the router plate. I drilled the track and secured it to the top with ⅝" screws. The track is available through most woodworking supply stores.

STEP 21 The T-track, which will be used to lock the adjustable fence, is also attached to the top in grooves. Rout the grooves on each side, parallel to the plate, and match the size of track you purchased, making sure they are flush with the tabletop surface. Once again, the tracks are secured with ⅝" screws.

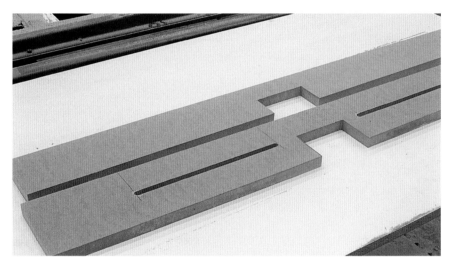

STEP 22 All of the fence parts are made with ¾"-thick MDF. The fence back rail BB has two ⅜"-wide grooves routed into the center and through the board. The grooves start 6" from each end and stop 16" from each end. This rail also requires a 4"-wide by 2½"-high notch, centered on the length of the board. The horizontal support CC also has a notch that is 4" wide by 2" high in the center of the board. Both notches can be cut with a band saw or jigsaw.

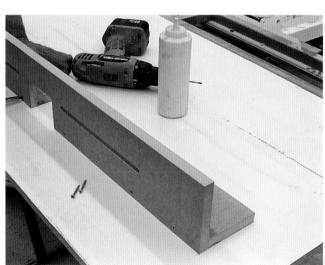

STEP 23 Attach the fence back rail BB to the horizontal support CC with 1½" screws and glue at about 4" on center.

STEP 24 The four right-angle fence supports DD are 4" x 4" blocks of ¾" MDF cut at 45°. Use glue and 1½" screws to attach the supports to the fence assembly. One support is installed at either end and the remaining two on each side of the cutout notch in the fence boards.

STEP 25 The back cover EE for the fence cutout has a 45° miter on both ends. Apply glue to all edges and secure the cover with a few brad nails on the top and bottom edge.

STEP 26 Drill a 2¼"-diameter hole in the center of the back cover. This will be used to friction-fit a vacuum hose.

STEP 27 Center the fence assembly on the router table and drill two ⅜"-diameter holes in the horizontal support over the center of each T-track. Use a T-nut and knob with a 1"-long by ¼"-diameter threaded shaft screwed into the nut. Tighten the knobs and verify that the fence locks securely.

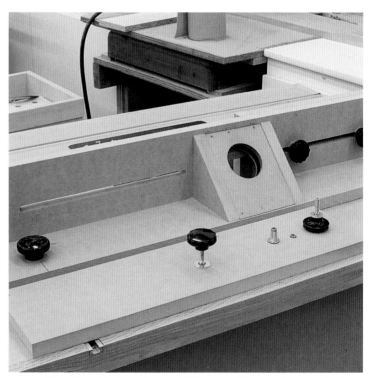

STEP 28 The adjustable fence boards FF have two T-nuts driven into the front faces. Counterbore the hole so the nuts are slightly below the fence face. Position the nuts so both fences can come together in the center and travel about 4" out from the center.

STEP 29 I will be using base option #2, as illustrated. Two pads KK are glued together and attached to the bottom, 3" back from the front edge of the cabinet and on both back corners. Drill holes for ¼"-diameter T-nuts and install a threaded metal foot in the center of each block as shown.

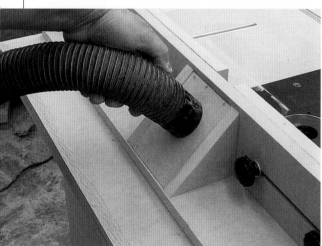

STEP 30 My 2¼"-outside-diameter vacuum hose on my shop vacuum is a snug fit in the dust hole and provides good particle removal.

STEP 31 I purchased and attached a construction-grade power bar, made by Belkin Components, called a SurgeMaster HD. This device is designed to control electrical equipment such as saws, compressors and routers. The vacuum cleaner and router will be plugged into the power bar and controlled by a switch. I will also have spare plugs that are overload protected, which I can use in the shop for other electrical equipment.

CONSTRUCTION
notes

You will need four sheets of ¾"-thick MDF to build this cabinet. I used about 13' of hardwood to edge the top, as well.

I used MDF, but any ¾" sheet material will be fine, and the same construction dimensions and procedures can be used. If you decide to use another material, look for a smooth surface so your router work will slide easily on the top.

Pay special attention to the final height of your cabinet. My cabinet, with the adjustable legs in base option #2, puts my top surface at about 35" above the floor. That's a comfortable height for me, but your requirements may be different. Adjust the vertical divider heights to meet your needs.

All of the aluminum track, knobs and related hardware are sold at most woodworking stores. Woodworkers tend to make jigs and shop-built tool accessories, so this line of hardware has become very popular.

I considered adding a dust collection port in the router compartment, but the dust doesn't seem to be that great a problem. My vacuum pulls most of the dust at the fence; however, routing a material that creates fine dust may cause a buildup in the compartment. If that's the case, drilling a dust port and making a Y-fitting so the vacuum could collect from the fence and router compartment would be an easy fix.

Drill Press Center

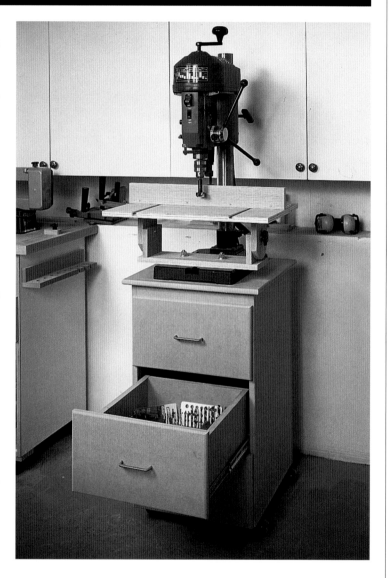

A drill press is a valuable asset in any woodworking shop. Drill presses are available as floor or bench models and have adjustable tables or heads. However, they all lack storage space and have tables that are difficult to adjust.

I built the storage cabinet portion of this project to be used with both floor and bench drill presses. The bench model can be bolted to the top, or the cabinet can be wheeled over the base on floor-model units. If you do own a floor-model press, measure the width and height of the base to be sure the cabinet can be rolled over the base. If the base is too large, change the cabinet dimensions to suit your drill press.

The full-extension top cabinet drawer can hold drill bits on an indexed board, while the remaining drawers can contain accessories, literature and other tools used with your drill press. If you need the drill press table on your floor-model unit lower than the cabinet height, simply roll it out of the way. Bench-model presses can be mounted on the top, and the station, both cabinet and drill press, can be rolled to any area of your shop.

Many woodworkers will appreciate the wide adjustable table. It can be tipped for angular drilling to the front or rear of your drill press. The adjustable fence is an important option that is missing on most drill units. Woodworkers use drill press fences a great deal and often have to clamp a straight-edged board to the press table. This fence is adjustable, easily locked in place and quick to move where needed.

The drill press center is easy to build, inexpensive and well worth the time. It's a great workstation to use, and I'm sure you'll quickly appreciate its value.

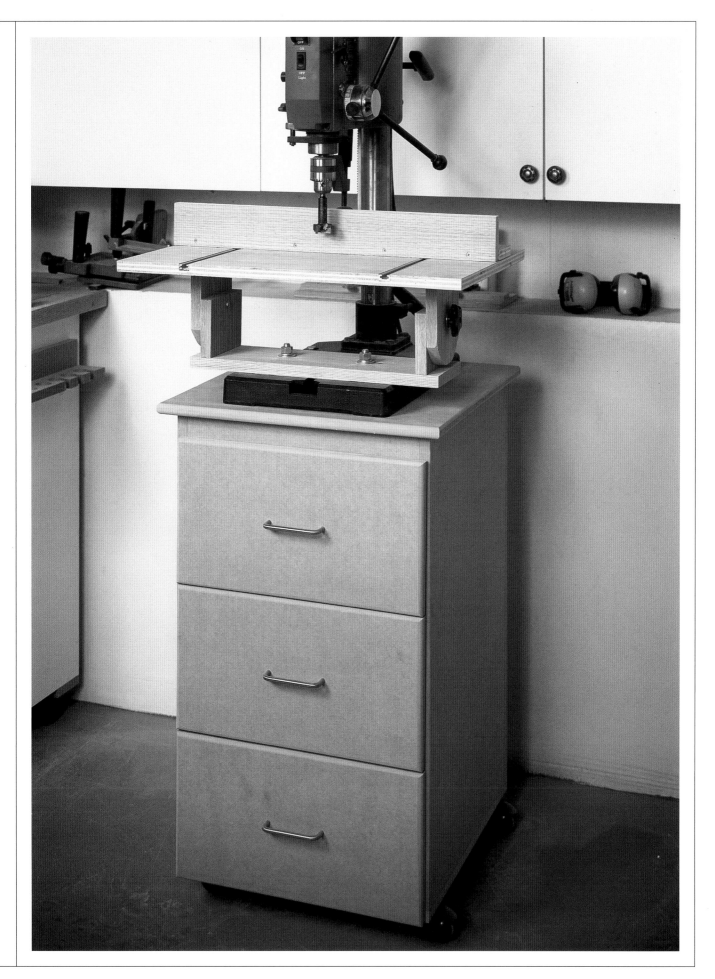

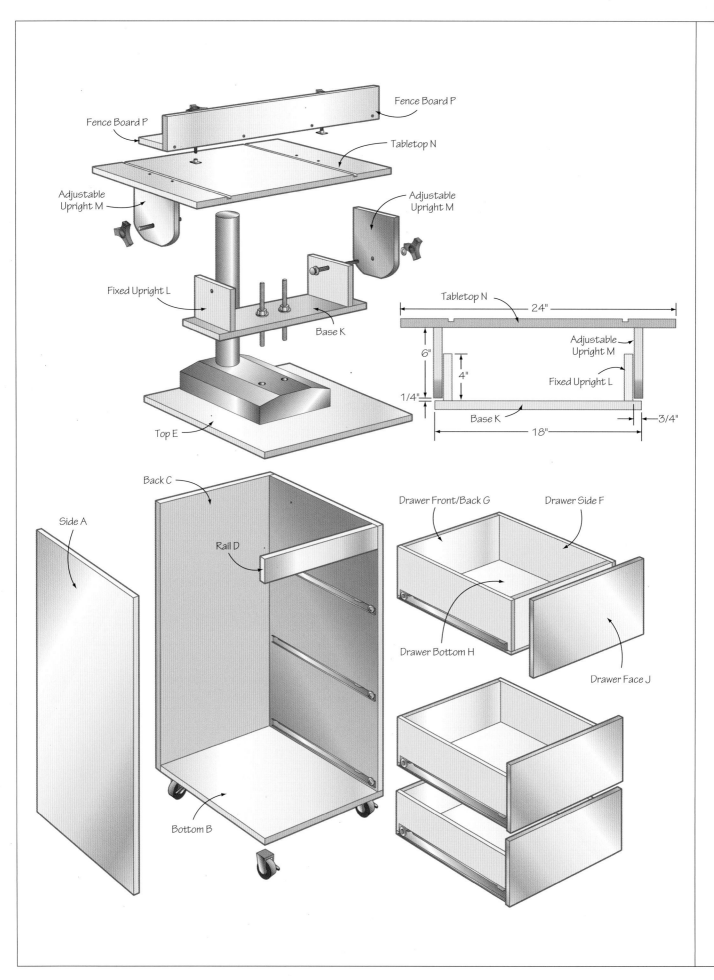

Fence Board P

Fence Board P

Tabletop N

Adjustable
Upright M

Adjustable
Upright M

Fixed Upright L

Base K

Tabletop N

24"

6"

4"

Adjustable
Upright M

Fixed Upright L

1/4"

Base K

3/4"

18"

Top E

Back C

Drawer Front/Back G

Drawer Side F

Side A

Rail D

Drawer Bottom H

Drawer Face J

Bottom B

Schedule of Materials: Drill Press Center

LTR.	NO.	ITEM	STOCK	INCHES T	(MM) T	INCHES W	(MM) W	INCHES L	(MM) L
Cabinet									
A	2	sides	MDF	¾	19	19	483	30	762
B	1	bottom	MDF	¾	19	18	457	19	483
C	1	back	MDF	¾	19	18	457	30¾	781
D	1	rail	MDF	¾	19	2	51	16¾	425
E	1	top	MDF	¾	19	20	508	21	533
F	6	drawer sides	MDF	¾	19	6¼	158	18	457
G	6	drawer fronts & backs	MDF	¾	19	6¼	158	14	356
H	3	drawer bottoms	MDF	¾	19	15½	394	18	457
J	3	drawer faces	MDF	¾	19	9⅝	245	17½	445
Adjustable Drill Table									
K	1	base	hardwood	¾	19	5¼	133	18	457
L	2	fixed uprights	hardwood	¾	19	5¼	133	4	102
M	2	adjustable uprights	hardwood	¾	19	5¼	133	6	152
N	1	tabletop	veneer ply	¾	19	16	406	24	610
P	2	fence boards	veneer ply	¾	19	3	76	24	610
Q	2	drill platforms	MDF	¾	19	14	356	16¾	425

Supplies - inches

Screws as detailed

Glue

3 Drawer handles

3 Sets of full-extension drawer glides

Right-angle brackets

Bolts and nuts as detailed

T-track

T-nuts

Knobs

1½" Screws

⅝" Screws

1¼" Screws

4 Wheels

2" Screws

¼" Carriage bolts with washer and knobs

½" Screws

¼" x 20 Bolt and knob assembly with 1"-long shaft

Supplies - metric

Screws as detailed

Glue

3 Drawer handles

3 Sets of full-extension drawer glides

Right-angle brackets

Bolts and nuts as detailed

T-track

T-nuts

Knobs

38mm Screws

16mm Screws

32mm Screws

4 Wheels

51mm Screws

6mm Carriage bolts with washer and knobs

13mm Screws

6mm x 20 Bolt and knob assembly with 25mm-long shaft

STEP 2 The back C is attached to the cabinet sides and bottom board with 1½" screws and glue. A properly cut back will square the cabinet.

STEP 1 Cut the two sides A and bottom board B to size as detailed in the materials list. Attach the bottom to the sides using 1½" screws, spaced 6" apart, and glue. Note that both sides rest on the bottom board, and the screws are installed on the underside of the bottom, into the edges of the side boards. Remember to drill pilot holes for the screws.

STEP 3 Cut and attach the top rail D using right-angle brackets and ⅝" screws. Apply glue to the rail ends and clamp securely when installing the brackets. The brackets are also installed on the sides, back and rail boards, and will be used to secure the cabinet top board.

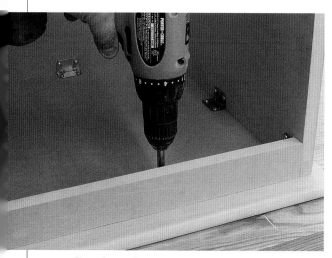

STEP 4 Round over the two sides and front edges of the top board E using a ⅜" roundover bit in a router. Use ⅝" screws in the right-angle brackets to secure the top. There should be a 1" overhang on both sides and a 1¼" overhang at the front edge. The top's back edge is aligned flush with the back face of the backboard.

STEP 5 The drawer boxes are 7" high by 15½" wide by 18" deep. I made my drawer boxes using the same ¾"-thick MDF as was used to build the cabinet carcass.

Cut the drawer box parts F, G and H to size. Begin the assembly by attaching the sides to the back and front boards using 1½" screws and glue. Two screws per joint, making sure the screws are kept 1" away from the tops and bottoms of the boards, will secure the joints.

STEP 6 The bottom boards are also attached to the side, back and front boards using 1½" screws and glue.

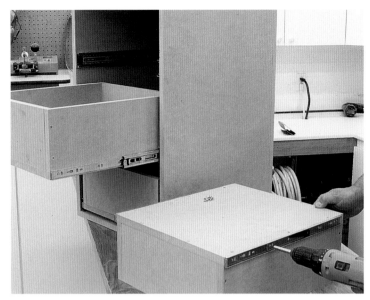

STEP 7 I used 18" full-extension drawer glides to mount my drawer boxes. The bottom drawer is installed as close to the bottom board as possible. The remaining two drawer boxes are installed leaving a 2" space between them.

STEP 8 The drawer faces J are 9⅝" high by 17½" wide using ¾" MDF. The front edges are rounded over with a ⅜" bit in a router. The bottom drawer face is aligned flush with the bottom edge of the cabinet base board and spaced ⅛" apart. Secure the faces to the drawer boxes using 1¼" screws from inside the drawer box. Attach handles or knobs of your choice.

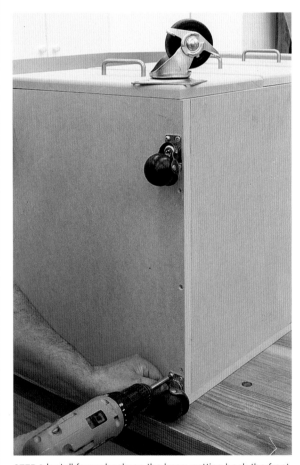

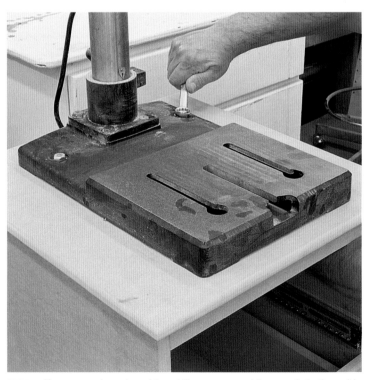

STEP 9 Install four wheels on the base, setting back the front set by 2". Use medium- or heavy-duty wheels, making sure they are high enough to straddle the drill press base if you own a floor model.

STEP 10 If you are using a benchtop drill press, mount it securely to the cabinet top with bolts or screws. If you own a floor-model press, you can skip this step.

STEP 11 Using hardwood, cut the table base K and the two fixed uprights L to size. Secure both uprights to the base K with glue and 2" screws. The uprights are attached ¾" in from each end of the base K.

STEP 12 Prepare the two adjustable uprights M by cutting them to the size indicated. Remove both lower corners on each board with a 45° cut that's 1½" from each end. Round over the corners with a belt sander, creating an arc on the bottom edge of each upright.

STEP 13 Following the rough shaping with the belt sander, clamp the two uprights together and finish-sand so both have the same profile.

STEP 14 Place the adjustable uprights M on the outside faces of each fixed upright L, aligning the edges of all boards. Use a ¼"-thick spacer under the adjustable uprights and drill a ¼"-diameter hole 3" down from their top edges through both boards. Center the hole on the width of each board and insert a ¼"-diameter carriage bolt, a large washer on the outside face and a knob to lock the uprights together.

STEP 15 Bolt the assembly to the table on your drill press. Each model will have different bolt hole patterns, so choose a method that suits your drill press table. Align the drill chuck center to the center of the table base board and tighten securely.

STEP 16 The tabletop N is a piece of ¾"-thick veneer plywood. Form two dadoes along the width of the board, 5" in from each edge. The T-track I'm using requires ⅜"-deep dadoes, but your hardware may be different, so verify the track depth before cutting the dadoes. Cut the tracks to length and secure them in the dadoes using ½" screws in countersunk holes at the bottom of the tracks.

STEP 17 Attach the top to the adjustable uprights using two 2" screws per upright. Align the top so it's equally spaced on both upright edges, side to side and back to front. Don't use glue in case the top has to be replaced in the future.

STEP 18 The fence is made with ¾"-thick veneer plywood. The horizontal and vertical members P are 3" high by 24" long. Attach the vertical board to the horizontal member with glue and four 2" screws. This simple but strong fence can be easily replaced if necessary.

STEP 19 Drill two ¼"-diameter holes in the horizontal fence board over the center of each T-track slot. To lock the fence, use a ¼" x 20 bolt and knob assembly with a 1"-long shaft screwed to T-nuts in the track.

STEP 20 I'm using one of the drawers, on full-extension drawer glides, to store and index my drill bits. Cut a piece of ¾" MDF to size for a drill platform Q. Drill the appropriate holes to store your bits and loosely sit the platform in the drawer box. New holes can be drilled as your bit inventory increases.

CONSTRUCTION
notes

If you build the drill press center as detailed, you'll need about 1¼ sheets of MDF, a 2' x 2' piece of veneer-covered plywood and a 40"-long piece of 1x6 hardwood. The hardware is available at most woodworking stores.

Many configurations are possible for the cabinet, and the final dimensions will depend on the size of your drill press. The sizes shown in this project should be suitable for the majority of floor and benchtop drill presses.

Any ¾" sheet material can be used. I decided to use MDF because it's inexpensive, can be easily worked with standard woodworking tools, doesn't require edge finishing and is a stable material. However, particleboard or plywood can be substituted if one of them is a personal favorite of yours.

An additional knob and bolt can be added to double-lock each set of uprights. If you do a lot of heavy work on the drill press, you might want some added insurance that the table will remain level, so add another ¼" x 20 bolt and knob to each side. Remove the extra lock when adjustments to the table are needed. However, the one-knob-per-side setup securely locks the table, and it would take quite a bit of weight to move it.

You may want to drill a large round hole in the table to insert a sanding drum. The drum can be installed in the drill chuck and lowered through the hole. The large table and a drum will make a great power sanding accessory. Dozens of drill press accessories are available, such as planers, plug cutters, hollow chisel mortise attachments and so on. The cabinet can be made with one drawer over a door with adjustable shelves or, as shown, three drawers on full-extension (FX) glides. The FX glides are the most expensive part of the project. To reduce costs, use an FX glide set on the drill bit drawer and bottom-mount glides on the others.

Tool Sharpening and Maintenance Station

Sharpening equipment is a necessity in every woodworking shop. Dull tools are aggravating to work with and dangerous. Keeping chisels, turning tools, plane blades and carving tools in good condition is a fact of life in the woodshop.

Many woodworkers use water stones and water-wheel grinders. The stones have to be kept wet to work effectively, so that means a water bath. However, woodworking tools create dust, and when mixed with water, a brown sludge forms in the water bath. Those of you who use oil stones have the same problem with dust — a brown paste covering the stones and lapping plates. I'm sure I've spent more time cleaning the stones and water baths than on actual tool maintenance.

I decided to build a dedicated sharpening station for my 1" belt sander, wet and dry wheel grinder and water bath for my stones. But I vowed to solve the dust and water problems with this station. The flip-up cover is my answer for a dust-free center, and it works great!

This project may not look sleek and stylish, but it keeps my water baths and stones "paste free" and saves me a great deal of time previously wasted cleaning the-equipment.

The power cords are routed through the top and plug into a power bar. Two large drawers provide all the space I need for sharpening accessories, extra blades for my tools and manuals related to my equipment. The section below the drawers is enclosed with doors for added dust-free storage. The station is mounted on locking wheels that allow me to bring it to any area in my shop.

If you want clean, almost dust-free sharpening equipment that's ready to use, then this project is for you. The cabinet won't win any beauty awards, but it's number one in the functional category.

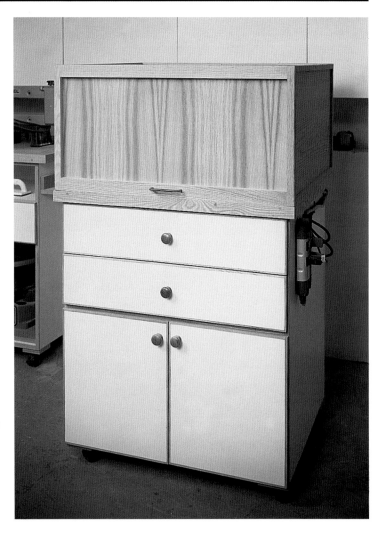

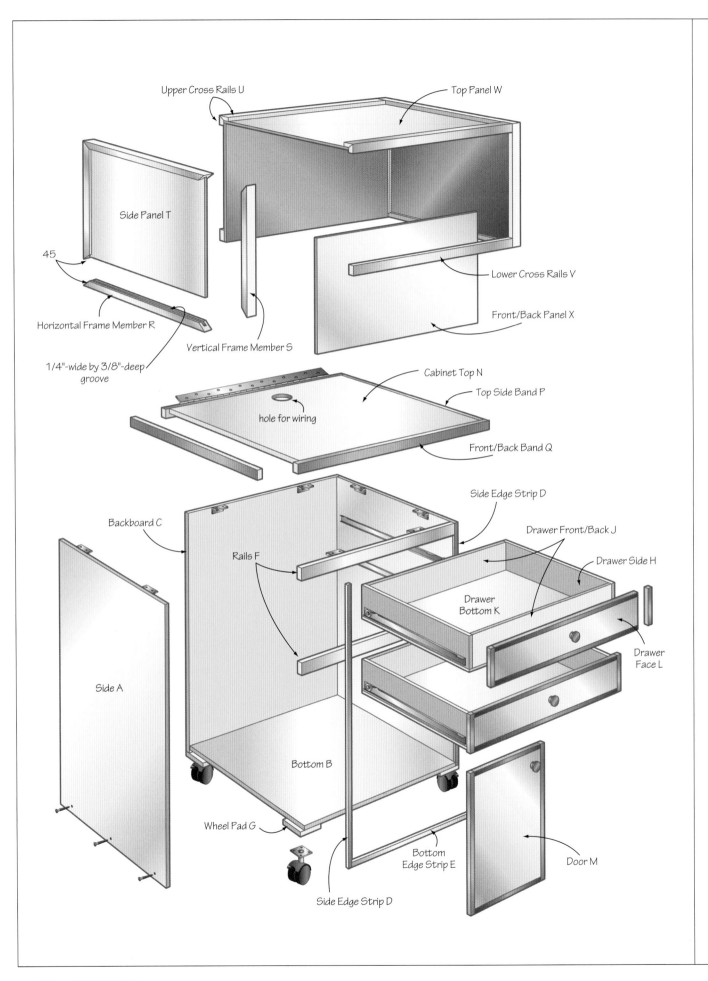

Upper Cross Rails U

Top Panel W

Side Panel T

45

Horizontal Frame Member R

Vertical Frame Member S

1/4"-wide by 3/8"-deep groove

Lower Cross Rails V

Front/Back Panel X

Cabinet Top N

Top Side Band P

hole for wiring

Front/Back Band Q

Backboard C

Side Edge Strip D

Drawer Front/Back J

Rails F

Drawer Side H

Drawer Bottom K

Side A

Drawer Face L

Bottom B

Wheel Pad G

Bottom Edge Strip E

Side Edge Strip D

Door M

Schedule of Materials: Tool Sharpening and Maintenance Station

LTR.	NO.	ITEM	STOCK	INCHES T	(MM) T	INCHES W	(MM) W	INCHES L	(MM) L	COMMENTS
Cabinet										
A	2	sides	melamine PB	⅝	16	23⅜	594	32	813	
B	1	bottom	melamine PB	⅝	16	23⅜	594	28¾	730	
C	1	backboard	melamine PB	⅝	16	30	762	32	813	
D	2	side edge strips	hardwood	¼	6	⅝	16	32	813	
E	1	bottom edge strip	hardwood	¼	6	⅝	16	28¾	730	
F	2	rails	hardwood	¾	19	1½	38	28¾	730	
G	4	wheel pads	hardwood	¾	19	3½	89	3½	89	
H	4	drawer sides	melamine PB	⅝	16	4⅜	112	22	559	
J	4	drawer fronts & backs	melamine PB	⅝	16	4⅜	112	26½	673	
K	2	drawer bottoms	melamine PB	⅝	16	22	559	27¾	705	
L	2	drawer faces	melamine PB	⅝	16	6½	165	29¾	756	
M	2	doors	melamine PB	⅝	16	14⅞	378	17½	445	
N	1	cabinet top	melamine PB	⅝	16	30¼	768	26½	673	
P	2	top side bands	hardwood	¾	19	1½	38	26½	673	
Q	2	front & back bands	hardwood	¾	19	1½	38	31¾	806	
Cover										
R	4	horizontal frame members	hardwood	¾	19	1	25	28	711	angle-cut
S	4	vertical frame members	hardwood	¾	19	1	25	16	406	angle-cut
T	2	side panels	veneer ply	¼	6	15¼	387	27¼	692	
U	4	upper cross rails	hardwood	¾	19	1½	38	29¾	756	angle-cut
V	2	lower cross rails	hardwood	¾	19	1½	38	29¾	756	
W	1	top panel	veneer ply	¼	6	30⅜	772	26⅜	670	
X	2	front & back panels	veneer ply	¼	6	30⅜	772	14¼	362	

Supplies - inches

8   Metal right-angle brackets

2" PB screws as detailed

Brad nails as detailed

Glue

White screw head cover caps as detailed

4   Locking wheels

Iron-on edge tape

2   22" Drawer glide sets

4   Knobs

4   107° Hidden hinges

1   28" Piano hinge

12" Length of small chain

1   Handle

1   Wire grommet

Metal angle brackets

Pocket screws

1¼" Screws

⅝" Screws

1" Screws

½" Screws

Biscuits

Wood plugs

Wire protector

Supplies - metric

8   Metal right-angle brackets

51mm PB screws as detailed

Brad nails as detailed

Glue

White screw head cover caps as detailed

4   Locking wheels

Iron-on edge tape

2   559mm Drawer glide sets

4   Knobs

4   107° Hidden hinges

1   711mm Piano hinge

305mm Length of small chain

1   Handle

1   Wire grommet

Metal angle brackets

Pocket screws

32mm Screws

16mm Screws

25mm Screws

6mm Screws

Biscuits

Wood plugs

Wire protector

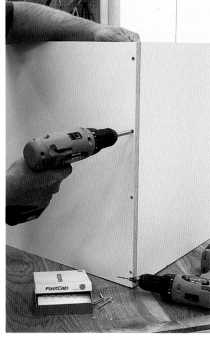

STEP 1 Join the sides A to the bottom board B by drilling 2" PB screws in pilot holes. Cover the screw heads with white stick-on caps or plastic covers.

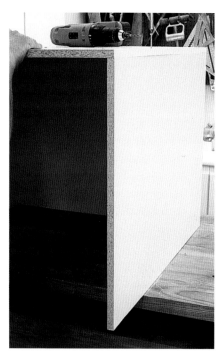

STEP 2 Apply iron-on edge tape to both long vertical edges of backboard C. Attach the back to the sides and bottom board using 2"-long PB screws.

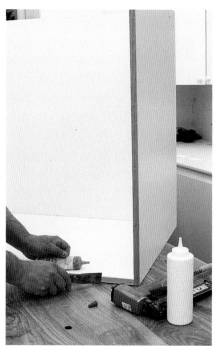

STEP 3 Glue and nail the solid-wood edge strips D and E to the front edges of the side and bottom boards. Fill the nail holes and sand smooth. I'm using oak hardwood for all my edge trim, but any solid wood can be used.

STEP 4 Cut and install the two wood rails F. Secure them to the cabinet with metal angle brackets, screws through the cabinet's side or, as I'm using, pocket screws. The top rail is flush with the top edges of the cabinet sides, and the middle rail is 13½" below the top edges. There should be a 12"-high opening between the two rails for the drawers.

STEP 5 Install the eight right-angle brackets that will be used to secure the cabinet top board. The brackets are attached flush with the top edges of the side, backboard and upper rail. I installed two brackets on each panel and two on the rail.

STEP 6 The four wood wheel pads G can be installed using 1" screws through the bottom board into the pads. They should be installed under the edges of the back and side boards so the load on those panels will shift through the pads and wheels to the floor. Four screws per pad will hold them securely to the cabinet bottom. The locking wheels are attached with 1¼" screws. The wheels I used are 2½" high, and including the pads, the cabinet is 3¼" off the floor.

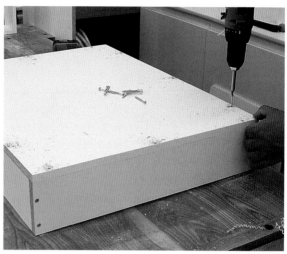

STEP 7 The two drawer boxes are 5" high by 27¾" wide. Cut all drawer parts H, J and K to size. I used ⅝"-thick melamine and secured the butt joints with 2" PB screws. Before assembling the boxes use iron-on edge tape to cover the top edges of the back, front and side boards, as well as the side edges of the bottom board. Attach the sides to the back and front boards using two screws per joint. Keep the screws at least 1" away from the edges of all boards to avoid splitting.

STEP 8 The drawer box bottom board is attached to the bottom edges of the side, back and front boards with 2" PB screws.

STEP 10 The drawer faces L are secured to the boxes with four 1" screws. Leave a ¹⁄₁₆" space between the upper and lower drawer face. I used ⅝"-thick melamine PB trimmed with ¼"-thick oak hardwood for my faces. You can use any material to make the drawer faces and doors as long as the finished sizes are the same as the dimensions detailed in the materials list. The drawer faces will overlap the top and middle rail by approximately ½".

STEP 9 Install the drawer boxes in the cabinet using 22" bottom-mount or, if you prefer, full-extension side-mount glides. The top glides are installed so the bottom of the top drawer box will be 5¾" below the lower edge of the top rail. Use ⅝" screws and follow the installation instructions that come with your hardware.

STEP 12 Drill two 35mm holes in each door, 3" on center from each end. The flat-bottomed hinge holes are drilled ⅛" in from the door's edge.

STEP 11 The door width is calculated by measuring the cabinet's inside width and adding 1". Since I want two doors on my cabinet, I will divide that number by two, (28¾" plus 1" divided by 2), which means I'll need both doors to be 14⅞" wide. The doors are installed flush with the lower edge of the bottom board and overlay the middle rail by about ⅜". I trimmed my door edges with oak, but as mentioned earlier, any material can be used as long as the overall dimensions of the doors are as stated in the materials list.

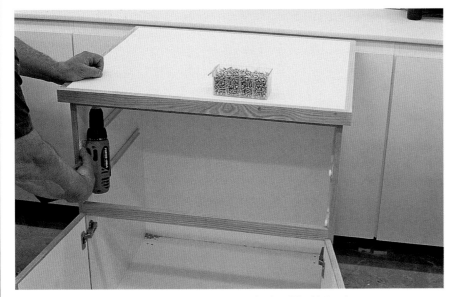

STEP 13 Install two standard-opening hinges (between 100° and 120°) in each door and secure them with ½"-long screws, making sure the hinges are 90° to the door's edge. Attach the hinge plates to the hinge body and hold the door against the cabinet in its normally open position with a ⅛" spacer between the door and cabinet edge. Drive screws through the hinge-plate holes to secure the door. Remove the spacer and test the door alignment. Install handles or knobs on the drawers and doors.

STEP 14 The cabinet top N is a sheet of ⅝"-thick melamine PB with hard-wood edge-banding. Attach the edge-banding P and Q with glue and biscuits or screws with wood plugs. Install the top with ⅝" screws through the metal brackets previously installed. There should be a ⅞" overhang on each side, a 1¼" overhang on the front edge and a 2½" overhang at the back edge. The larger overhang on the back will be used to install a wire hole and grommet.

STEP 15 Drill a wire hole in the back of the top, 1" from the rear edge. Use a wire protector (commonly found at stores that sell electronic supplies). The power cords can pass through the hole and be attached to a power bar.

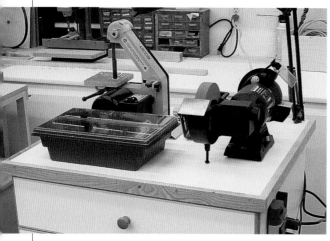

STEP 16 Install your sharpening tools on the cabinet top, keeping them 1" from any edge. I have a 1" belt sander, wet and dry wheel grinder, a water stone bath and a magnifying lamp. I also attached a power bar made by Stanley Tools on the cabinet side. Your equipment will be different from mine, but it should be installed at this time to determine the minimum inside height of the cover.

STEP 17 My cover is the full width and depth of the top, so I need 15" of inside clearance based on my equipment. The side frame will be made with hardwood that's 1" wide by ¾" thick. Both ends on frame members R and S are cut at 45° to create a mitered corner at each intersection. The side panels will be ¼"-thick veneer plywood.

Cut a groove that's ¼" wide on one 1" face of each horizontal and vertical ⅜"-deep frame member. Miter the ends of each member so the long edge is the dimension stated in the materials list. The grooves are on the inside, short dimension of each mitered board. Assemble the two side frames with the panels T installed in the grooves. Use glue and brad nails, then clamp securely until the adhesive cures.

STEP 18 Prepare the four upper cross rails U by ripping a 45° miter along one edge of each board. The face of these rails should be 1½" wide after ripping the angle. Create a back-and-front upper cross rail assembly by gluing the boards together in pairs at the miter. You should have two assemblies that form a right angle. The boards can be glued and brad nailed or clamped. If you use brads, keep them ⅜" back from the corner intersection so the edges can be rounded with a router bit.

STEP 19 Join the two sides with the upper cross rails using glue and 2" screws in counterbored holes. These holes can be filled with wood plugs. One 2" screw and glue at each joint will securely hold the rails to the sides.

STEP 20 The two lower cross rails V are also secured with glue and one 2" screw at each end. Counterbore and fill the screw holes with wood plugs.

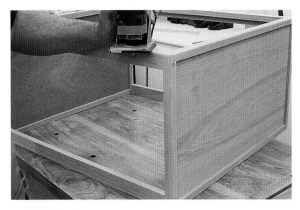

STEP 21 Use a ¼" roundover bit to ease all the outside edges of the frame members. Do not round over the bottom edges of the cover, because it should sit tight and flat on the cabinet top.

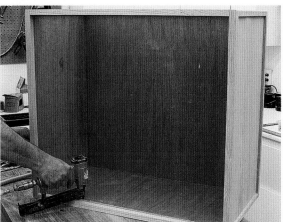

STEP 22 The top panel W and front and back panels X are attached to the inside of the cover with glue and ⅝" brad nails.

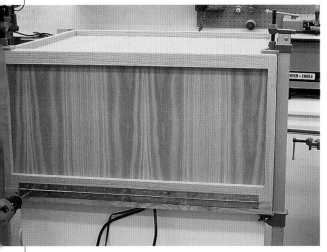

STEP 23 Clamp the cover in place on the cabinet so its edges are flush with the outside edges of the top. Use a 28" piano hinge on the back side to secure the cover to the cabinet.

STEP 24 Use a small chain about 12" long to limit the travel of the cover. Then install a handle on the front lower cross rail of the cover so it can be easily raised and lowered.

CONSTRUCTION
notes

You need to deal with two important issues before beginning construction of this sharpening station. First, decide on a comfortable work-surface height and, if it is different from mine, change the height of the sides and backboard to suit your requirements.

Second, the type of equipment that will be mounted on this station will determine the size of the top and clearance requirements for the cover. The belt sander is normally the tallest piece of equipment and is the unit that determines the cover height.

I built my station using ⅝"-thick particleboard and oak hardwood for the trim; however, any sheet material will work just as well. If you do use another sheet material such as MDF or plywood, consider installing a melamine PB or high-pressure laminate top. A smooth surface that's easy to clean is a real bonus.

You may also want to put a self-adhesive foam or rubber gasket on the bottom edge of the cover to further protect the equipment from dust. The cover can be built in another style, with other materials, but a ⅝"-thick melamine PB prototype that I built was very heavy to lift. The frame and panel cover is light and easy to manage, which convinced me that it was the best design for this application.

Finally, change the drawer and door compartments if they don't meet your needs. Three or four small drawers may be more suitable, or for some of you, one drawer will be fine. This project should be designed and built to accommodate your sharpening requirements.

Saw Outfeed Table and Storage Cabinet

For years my table saw outfeed table was part of a sheet of melamine particleboard (PB) supported by a pair of those inexpensive folding legs you can buy at a home store. The table wasn't very stable and could, and often did, move when I was cutting heavy sheet material on the saw. That safety issue alone made me look toward designing a better outfeed table.

Storage under the metal folding support legs was reduced because of their angle locking system. The legs weren't adjustable, so I was always leveling the table with small pieces of wood. It was a poor outfeed support system and something better, and safer, was needed.

This outfeed table and storage cabinet meets all of my needs. I built it using ¾"-thick MDF, so it's heavy and stable. It has an adjustable leg system, and the cabinet box provides a great deal of storage space. Adjustable shelves and doors allow me to customize the cabinet for my storage requirements.

The outfeed tabletop I need for my table saw is 3' wide by 6' long. Yours will most likely be different, so change the dimensions to suit your needs. The height will also be different for many of you, so adjust the vertical panel dimension. The cabinet top should be flush with your table saw top.

The cabinet height is a combination of top thickness, vertical panel length and adjustable leg height. If you plan on using an adjustable leg system, buy it before you start and note the height in the middle of the adjustment range. Then cut the side and center panels to the size required based on your table saw height.

The cabinet doesn't require doors if you plan on adding extra shelves to store short lengths of wood. You might want one section with doors for dust-free storage and the other without for small panel storage. There are many ways to configure the cabinet storage section based on your needs. No matter which storage setup you choose, you'll appreciate all the benefits of this solid outfeed table and storage center.

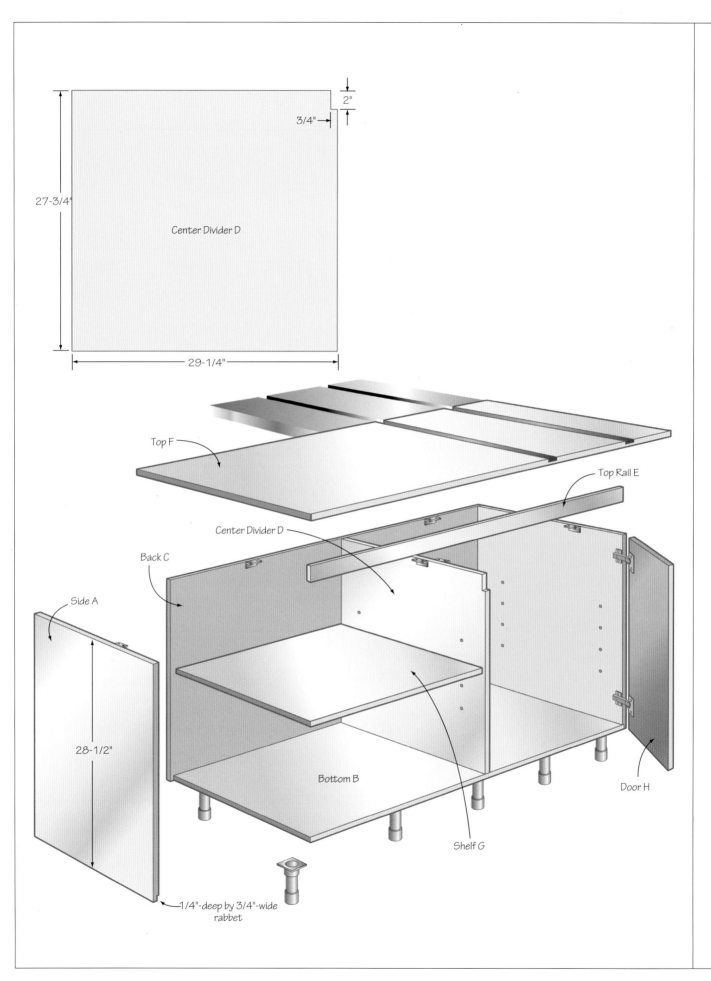

2"

3/4"

27-3/4"

Center Divider D

29-1/4"

Top F

Top Rail E

Center Divider D

Back C

Side A

28-1/2"

Bottom B

Shelf G

Door H

1/4"-deep by 3/4"-wide rabbet

Schedule of Materials:
Saw Outfeed Table and Storage Cabinet

LTR.	NO.	ITEM	STOCK	INCHES T	(MM) T	INCHES W	(MM) W	INCHES L	(MM) L
A	2	sides	MDF	¾	19	29¼	743	28½	724
B	1	bottom	MDF	¾	19	29¼	743	66½	1689
C	1	back	MDF	¾	19	28½	724	67½	1715
D	1	center divider	MDF	¾	19	29¼	743	27¾	705
E	1	top rail	MDF	¾	19	2	51	66	1676
F	1	top	MDF	¾	19	36	914	72	1829
G	2	shelves	MDF	¾	19	32⁹⁄₁₆	827	29	737
H	4	doors	MDF	¾	19	16⅝	422	27½	699

Supplies - inches

2" PB screws as detailed

⅝" Screws as detailed

Glue

11 Right-angle brackets

10 Adjustable legs

8 Shelf pins

4 107° Full-overlay hinges

4 107° Half-overlay hinges

8 Standard hinge plates

4 Door handles

⅝" Screws

Supplies - metric

51mm PB screws as detailed

16mm Screws as detailed

Glue

11 Right-angle brackets

10 Adjustable legs

8 Shelf pins

4 107° Full-overlay hinges

4 107° Half-overlay hinges

8 Standard hinge plates

4 Door handles

16mm Screws

STEP 1 Cut cabinet sides A to the dimensions listed in the materials list. Drill adjustable shelf-pin holes in the inside face of each side panel. Mark the top of each panel so the first hole distance is referenced from the top edge. This important step will ensure that the center divider's shelf-pin holes will be in alignment with the side panel holes.

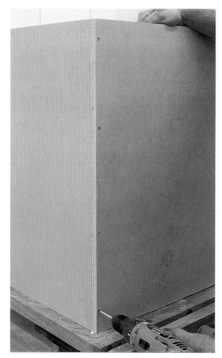

STEP 2 Both side panels require a rabbet that's ¼" deep by ¾" wide on their bottom inside edge. Next, cut the bottom board B to size and join the sides to the bottom board in the rabbets. The joints are secured with glue and four 2" screws on each panel. Remember to drill pilot holes for the screws.

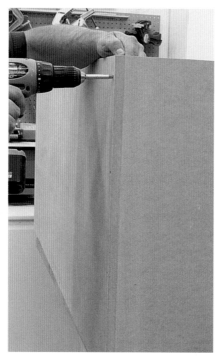

STEP 3 The back C fully overlays or covers the back edges of the sides and bottom board. Use glue and 2" screws, about 6" apart, to secure the back.

STEP 4 Drill a series of shelf-pin holes on each side of center divider D, being sure to mark and reference the first hole from the top edge of the panel. This will align the side and center divider shelf-pin holes.

Offset the columns of holes on each side of the panel by 1" to avoid drilling through the divider. On the top front edge of the panel, cut a notch that's ¾" deep by 2" high to receive the top rail. Secure the divider in the center of the cabinet, creating two sections that are 32⅝" wide. Use glue and screws through the back and bottom board to secure the divider.

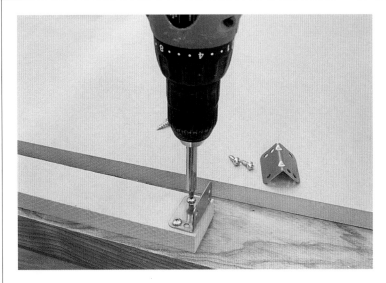

STEP 5 The top rail E is attached to the sides and in the notch of the center panel. The rail is only 2" wide, so screws driven in the end will usually split the MDF. I secured the rail with glue and right-angle brackets using ⅝" screws. Both ends of the rail are aligned with the side's top and face edges. The rail will be secured to the underside of the cabinet top with more right-angle brackets and screws.

STEP 6 The base support for my table is its adjustable legs. You might opt for a solid base, made with ¾" MDF, but most shop floors are uneven and the adjustable leg is an ideal solution. These legs are available at most woodworking stores.

Attach 10 legs using the manufacturer's fastening recommendations. Two legs are placed under each cabinet side board and two under the center divider. The other four are attached in the middle of each section span.

A base or leg system placed directly under the cabinet's vertical panels will properly transfer the cabinet load to the floor. Set the legs 2" back from the front edge of the cabinet to provide space when someone is standing at the front of the cabinet.

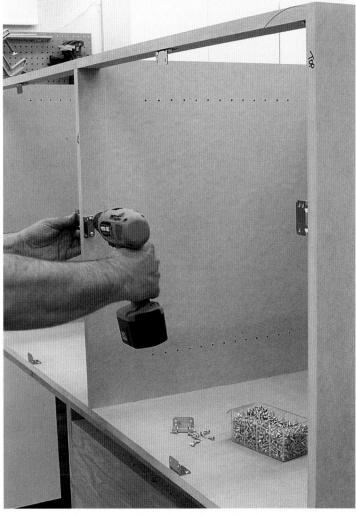

STEP 7 Attach eight right-angle brackets in the center of each panel and on the center of each rail span in every section. These brackets, which will be used to secure the cabinet top, should be flush with the top edge of each panel.

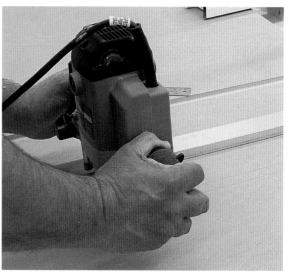

STEP 8 The top board F is ¾"-thick MDF. Secure it to the cabinet using screws through the previously installed brackets.

The sides overhang the cabinet by 2¼". The front overhang is 1", and the top extends past the back of the cabinet by 5". I've offset the front and back overhang so the cabinet won't interfere with my vacuum system behind the table saw. Adjust the top overhang to suit your shop setup.

STEP 9 Place the cabinet in its permanent location and level the top to the table saw top. Use a router and straightedge to cut two dadoes in the cabinet top that are in line with the miter slide tracks of the saw. Adjust the dado depth to match the track depth on the saw.

STEP 10 I installed two shelf boards G in my cabinet, but your storage needs may be different, so install as many as needed. The best shelf pin for this application has a full-metal shaft to support heavy loads. Install the pins in the drilled holes and test fit the shelves.

STEP 11 The cabinet can be left as an open shelving unit or have doors installed. The doors are attached using 100° to 120° hidden hinges. Cut the four doors H, then drill two 35mm-diameter holes in each that are 4" on center from each end and ⅛" away from the door edge. Hinge holes are approximately ½" deep, but test fit the hinges to ensure they are seated correctly.

STEP 12 The hinges on the two outside doors are full-overlay models, and the four on the inside doors are half-overlay. Install the hinges, with hinge plates attached, then mount the doors on the cabinets.

Hold the door in its normally open position, flush with the bottom edge of the base board. Place a ⅛"-thick strip of wood between the door edge and cabinet front edge. This spacing is needed to properly set the door-to-cabinet gap. Drive screws through the hinge-plate holes into the cabinet to secure the doors. Adjust the doors if necessary so there's a ¹⁄₁₆" gap in the center of each pair. Finally, install four handles of your choice.

CONSTRUCTION
notes

You can avoid using a combination of half- and full-overlay hinges by installing two center dividers. Follow the same installation steps for the second divider, being sure to leave equal spacing in both sections of the cabinet. You won't have to worry about offsetting shelf-pin hole columns with two dividers, and standard full-overlay hinges can be used on all the doors. Door width will change with the two-divider system, however. Measure the inside width of the cabinet, add 1" to that dimension and divide by 2; that's the required width of each door.

The cabinet interior is easily modified to suit your needs. Vertical dividers can be installed to create more than two sections, extra shelves can be added and doors can be installed on all or one section only. The cabinet can be easily customized for your shop.

If you plan on storing a lot of heavy items on the shelves, I suggest you use ¾"-thick plywood in place of the MDF. This two-section cabinet design requires wide shelves that can bend with heavy loads. If the shelves will be used to support heavy material or equipment, consider building the cabinet with three sections as a possible option.

As previously discussed, this cabinet design suits my table saw. Most saws are close in style and dimension, but you will have to make minor dimensional changes to suit your equipment. You might also consider mounting this cabinet on locking wheels if your table saw is mobile; however, you will need a level workshop floor for this option.

Cope-and-Stick Muntin-Cutting Fixture

Muntins used on cope-and-stick doors are small and delicate. They are often only 1" (25mm) wide and ½" (13mm) thick. These small parts are easily shattered and split by cope-and-stick router bits, and cutting them can be dangerous if they're not handled properly, so you have to be careful. Here's a simple fixture that will help you avoid problems when routing small parts.

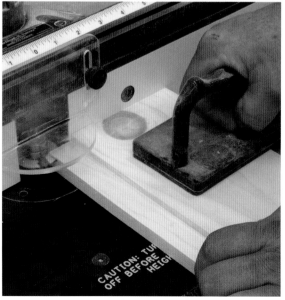

STEP ONE Align the router-table fence with the bearing on the cope bit so both the fence and the bearing guide the muntin in the same plane. Once the correct muntin length has been calculated, form the cope cuts on each end. Push the muntins through the cope bit with a wide backer board behind it. This board will provide a lot more surface area and stabilize the small muntins as they pass through the bit. Be sure the muntin is held tightly against the backer board.

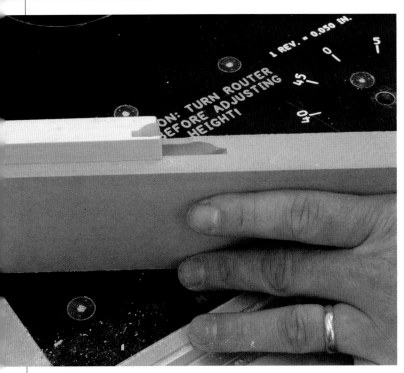

STEP TWO Before cutting the stick profiles on the muntins, cut a cope profile into the edge of a 4"-wide (102mm) piece of MDF, stopping 2" (51mm) from the end. This cope profile will hold the stick profile that will be formed on one edge of the muntin.

STEP THREE Switch to a stick bit and form one edge profile on each muntin. After making a test cut, turn off the router and place the profiled wood edge against the stick bit. Ensure that the outfeed fence on your router table will support the reduced width of the workpiece after cutting. If it doesn't align properly, shim or adjust the outfeed fence so the workpiece is supported by the infeed fence before the cut and the outfeed fence after cutting. The cutter bearings should be in line with the infeed fence for this operation.

STEP FOUR This is the point where problems arise when milling narrow muntins. Once the opposite stick profile is cut, there's very little flat material left on the muntin and it will tip on the router table — not a safe situation.

The previously coped MDF fixture board can support the already profiled edge of the muntin so the opposite side can be cut safely. Insert the muntin in the fixture and hold it securely against the router-table fence.

STEP FIVE The muntin is secure in the jig's cope cut and trapped tightly against the router fence. It can be pushed through the bit to cut the stick profile on the opposite edge of the muntin.

Dado Jig

Cutting dadoes is an easy task to perform with a router. This jig gives you the flexibility to regulate the width of dadoes and cut them quickly.

Supplies

4	Threaded knobs ¼-20
4	Carriage bolts ¼-20 x 2½" (64mm)
4	Flat washers ¼
1	Threaded rod ⁵⁄₁₆-18 x 7" (178mm)
2	Flat washers ⁵⁄₁₆
2	T-nuts ⁵⁄₁₆-18
5	Hex nuts ⁵⁄₁₆-18

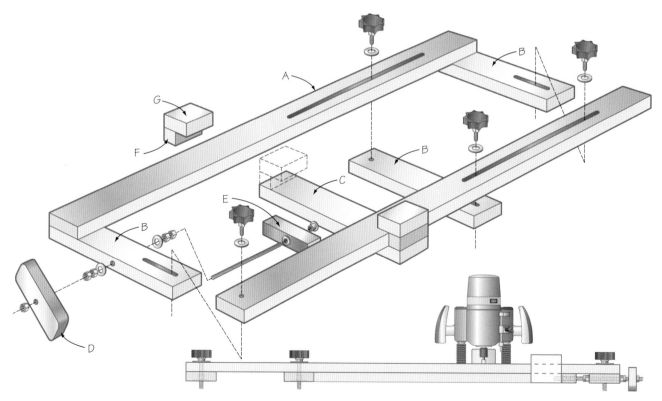

STEP ONE Begin by cutting the parts to size. Using a straight bit in a router mounted in a table, rout grooves in the parts that need them. (See the illustration.) Center the grooves in the parts.

Schedule of Materials: Dado Jig

LTR.	NO.	ITEM	STOCK	INCHES T	(MM) T	INCHES W	(MM) W	INCHES L	(MM) L
A	2	rails	½ plywood	1	25	2½	64	36	914
B	3	cross rails	½ plywood	1	25	2½	64	12	305
C	2	clamping rails	½ plywood	1	25	2½	64	14	356
D	4	handle	plywood	¾	19	1¼	32	5	127
E	2	pressure plate	plywood	¾	19	1½	38	5	127
F	2	guide spacers	½ plywood	1	25	1	25	2½	64
G	1	guide keepers	plywood	¾	19	2	51	2½	64

STEP TWO Drill a recess hole in the top and bottom of the pressure plate for the two T-nuts. Then drill a ⅜"-diameter (10mm) through-hole. This hole will house the shafts of the T-nuts and allow the threaded rod to pass through the plate. (See the illustration.) Then drill a through-hole in one of the end cross beams.

STEP THREE Cut a wider groove in the bottom of the cross beams directly beneath the ¼"-wide (6mm) groove for the bolts. This groove will house the head of the carriage bolt and recess it below the surface of the cross beam. Note the recess hole for the fixed carriage bolt.

STEP FOUR Using screws and glue, attach the top and the bottom (the one with the through-hole drilled in it) cross beams to one of the rails. Be sure that the cross beams are square with the rail.

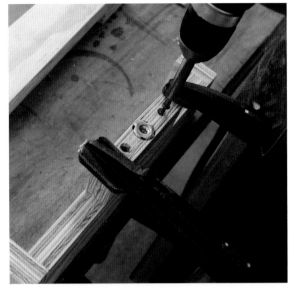

STEP FIVE Install the T-nuts in the pressure plate. Then test the fit of the opposing T-nuts by inserting the threaded rod into the T-nuts. If the rod binds slightly, adjust the depth of one of the T-nuts until the rod will thread through both nuts smoothly. Then, using glue and screws, attach the pressure plate to one of the slotted cross beams. When inserting screws into the end grain of plywood, predrill a hole a little larger than the diameter of the screw. Don't overtighten the screws. The glue will help hold the pressure plate securely.

STEP SIX Install the threaded rod into the pressure plate, and install a flat washer and two hex nuts on the rod. Tighten the nuts against one another so they lock together. Attach the spacer and guide blocks to the cross beam. Install the four carriage bolts, washers and threaded knobs.

STEP SEVEN Install a flat washer and two hex nuts on the threaded rod. Tighten the nuts against each other so they lock together.

STEP EIGHT Drill a $5/16$"-hole (8mm) in the handle and attach it to the end of the threaded rod, locking it in place between the two locked hex nuts and a final hex nut on the end of the rod. Tighten this nut securely so the handle is locked into place. When the handle is turned, the pressure plate and cross-beam assembly will move independently from the rest of the jig, enabling you to tighten the jig to your workpiece to hold it securely while you rout your dadoes.

Box-Squaring Fixture

Holding panels square and flush with each other during assembly while attempting to predrill or screw isn't always easy. This simple fixture will give you that extra hand needed to get started with case assembly.

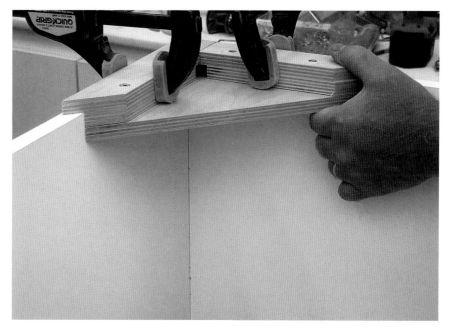

STEP ONE For each clamping jig, cut an 8" (203mm) x 8" (203mm) x ½" (13mm) piece of Baltic birch plywood. Adjust your miter saw to 45° and cut a triangle. It is well worth it to make several of these jigs.

STEP TWO For each clamping jig, cut two 1"-wide (25mm) strips to build up the sides. Glue the strips to the triangle and fasten them with brad nails or 1" (25mm) screws.

STEP THREE Add a layer of 1½"-wide (38mm) strips to create a ½" (13mm) lip on the outside of the jig. Drill a pilot hole with a countersink and secure with 1¼" (32mm) screws.

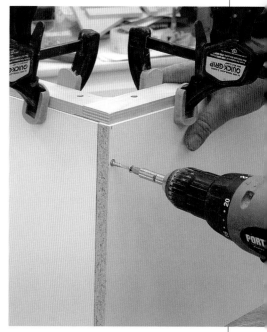

STEP FOUR To use the jig, bring together two project panels to make a butt joint. Clamp the fixture over one side of the panel, then make a butt joint to the other panel at 90°. Make them flush on the ends and the top.

45° Miter Clamp Jig

H ere is a fast and easy way to put together miters that will stay flat and square. The large base will allow you to glue wide or narrow stock.

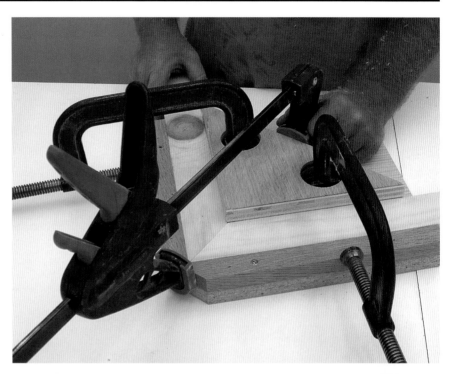

STEP ONE Cut a 12" x 12" (305mm x 305mm) piece of veneer plywood or particleboard. Add 1½"-wide (35mm) solid-wood cleats glued and screwed at the 90° corner.

STEP TWO Cut the back corner at 45° to allow a clamp to sit flat on the corner.

STEP THREE I glued two 8" (203mm) triangles together to create a 1½"-thick (38mm) corner block. Drill two 1½"-diameter (38mm) holes to accommodate clamp heads.

STEP FOUR To use the 45° miter clamp jig, bring together two mitered boards and clamp in place. You can also make a high-pressure laminate-covered version of this jig for easier clean up of glue squeeze-out.

Tapering Fixture

The thought of cutting angles on a table saw is not appealing at first, but using this fixture can make the process safer and more accurate. It will allow you to set different angles for your taper. You can build this fixture by modifying the Rough-Lumber Sawing Fixture made previously in this chapter.

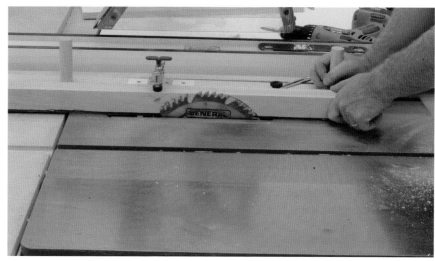

STEP ONE Remove the original 3"-wide (76mm) clamping board and replace it with a 1"-wide (25mm) strip of hardwood. Fix the strip to the Masonite carrier board using 1" (25mm) screws every 4" (102mm).

STEP TWO Reattach the clamping board to the fixed board using a butt hinge at the front of the inside edge, or simply add a 1" (25mm) screw from the underside that will act as a pivot point.

STEP THREE To lock the angle in place, I used a lid stay. Drill a hole 8" (203mm) from the end through the adjustable board and drive in a T-nut. The hole may need to be counterbored so that the T-nut sits flush with the face of the board. The threaded knob is then used to lock the lid stay in place. The angle bracket is simply fastened to the fixed board with ⅝" (16mm) screws.

Danny Proulx

For over 15 years, Danny shared with us his passion for woodworking through his books, magazine articles and website advice, as well as through teaching and mentoring his students and clients. He founded Rideau Cabinet in 1989 and started building kitchens and specialty cabinets. Over time, Danny married his love of woodworking and writing with his photographic skills and wrote 15 books during a period of 9 years. He also wrote for several magazines including *Popular Woodworking*, *Canadian Woodworking* and *Cabinet-Maker Magazine*. He started giving seminars in his home for new woodworkers and eventually started teaching courses at Algonquin College in Ottawa, Ontario.

In reviewing the projects to include in this collection, I was struck by the simplicity, practicality and thought that went into each of his designs. There's nothing especially fancy, but each project has little details to make them easier to use, more accurate, and often just simpler to build, each of which appealed to me as a woodworker and editor. We're proud to allow Danny's teaching legacy to live on in this and his other works.

- David Thiel, Editor

Metric Conversion Chart

TO CONVERT	TO	MULTIPLY BY
Inches	Centimeters	2.54
Centimeters	Inches	0.4
Feet	Centimeters	30.5
Centimeters	Feet	0.03
Yards	Meters	0.9
Meters	Yards	1.1

Distributed in Canada by Fraser Direct
100 Armstrong Avenue
Georgetown, Ontario L7G 5S4
Canada

Distributed in the U.K. and Europe by
F&W Media International, LTD
Brunel House, Ford Close
Newton Abbot
TQ12 4PU, UK
Tel: (+44) 1626 323200
Fax: (+44) 1626 323319
E-mail: enquiries@fwmedia.com

Distributed in Australia by Capricorn Link
P.O. Box 704, Windsor, NSW 2756 Australia
Tel: (02) 4560 1600; Fax: (02) 4577 5288
Email: books@capricornlink.com.au

Visit our website at popularwoodworking.com or our consumer website at shopwoodworking.com for more woodworking information projects.

Other fine Popular Woodworking Books are available from your local bookstore or direct from the publisher.

17   16   15   14   13   5   4   3   2   1

Acquisitions editor: David Thiel
Designer: Angela Wilcox
Production coordinator: Mark Griffin

Read This Important Safety Notice

To prevent accidents, keep safety in mind while you work. Use the safety guards installed on power equipment; they are for your protection.

When working on power equipment, keep fingers away from saw blades, wear safety goggles to prevent injuries from flying wood chips and sawdust, wear hearing protection and consider installing a dust vacuum to reduce the amount of airborne sawdust in your woodshop.

Don't wear loose clothing, such as neckties or shirts with loose sleeves, or jewelry, such as rings, necklaces or bracelets, when working on power equipment. Tie back long hair to prevent it from getting caught in your equipment.

People who are sensitive to certain chemicals should check the chemical content of any product before using it.

Due to the variability of local conditions, construction materials, skill levels, etc., neither the author nor Popular Woodworking Books assumes any responsibility for any accidents, injuries, damages or other losses incurred resulting from the material presented in this book.

The authors and editors who compiled this book have tried to make the contents as accurate and correct as possible. Plans, illustrations, photographs and text have been carefully checked. All instructions, plans and projects should be carefully read, studied and understood before beginning construction.

Prices listed for supplies and equipment were current at the time of publication and are subject to change.

Ideas. Instruction. Inspiration.

These and other great Popular Woodworking products are available at
your local bookstore, woodworking store or online supplier.

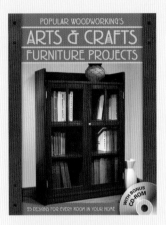

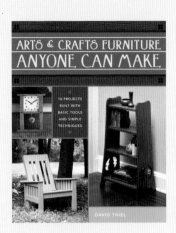

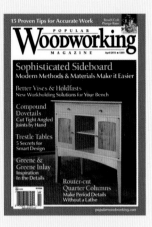

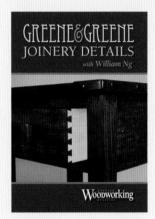

POPULAR WOODWORKING'S ARTS & CRAFTS FURNITURE PROJECTS

By The Popular Woodworking Staff

Arts & Crafts Furniture Projects focuses on popular pieces that are sure to appeal to woodworking enthusiasts of all levels. The bonus CD Rom includes additional projects not featured in the book, as well as useful tips and technique articles.

paperback · 208 pages

ARTS & CRAFTS FURNITURE ANYONE CAN MAKE

By David Thiel

Classic Arts & Crafts furniture designs are offerd as simple, screw-together projects so that anyone can build great-looking furniture. Using basic tools and home center lumber, even a first-time woodworker can successfully create a piece of furniture in a weekend.

paperback · 160 pages

POPULAR WOODWORKING MAGAZINE

Whether learning a new hobby or perfecting your craft, *Popular Woodworking Magazine* provides seven issues a year with the expert information you need to learn the skills, not just build the project. Find the latest issue on newsstands, or you can order online at popularwoodworking.com.

GREENE & GREENE JOINERY DETAILS DVD

By William Ng

In this DVD you will learn how to create five Greene & Green details, using jigs and simple techniques, providing a stunning finish to your next project.

 Available at shopwoodworking.com
DVD & Instant download

POPULAR WOODWORKING'S VIP PROGRAM
Get the Most Out of Woodworking!

Join the ShopWoodworking VIP program today for the tools you need to advance your woodworking abilities. Your one-year paid renewal membership includes:

· *Popular Woodworking Magazine* (1 year/7 issue U.S. subscription — a $21.97 value)

· *Popular Woodworking Magazine* CD — Get all issues of *Popular Woodworking Magazine* from 2006 to to 2010 (a $64.95 value!)

· *The Best of Shops & Workbenches* CD — 62 articles on workbenches, shop furniture, shop organization and essential jigs and fixtures (a $15 value)

· Roubo Plate 11 Poster — A beautiful 18" x 24" reproduction of Plate 11 from Andre Roubo's 18th-century masterpiece *L'Art du Menuisier,* on heavy, cream-colored stock

· 20% Members-Only Savings on 6-Month Subscription for ShopClass OnDemand

· 10% Members-Only Savings at Shopwoodworking.com

· 10% Members-Only Savings on FULL PRICE Registration for Woodworking In America Conference (Does Not Apply with Early Bird Price)

· and more....

Visit **popularwoodworking.com** to see more woodworking information by the experts, learn about our
digital subscription and sign up to receive our weekly newsletter at popularwoodworking.com/newsletters/
